Practical Ruby 3 Programming

Simpler than Python, offering concise syntax, reusable code, and maximum developer productivity

Zorin Fylix

Published by: GitforGits

Publisher: Sonal Dhandre

www.gitforgits.com

support@gitforgits.com

Printed in India

First Printing: December 2024

ISBN: 978-81-984316-8-4

Cover Design by: Kitten Publishing

Prologue

Why Ruby?

Well, for one thing, it's got a sleek and simple vibe that not many languages can match. When I first came across Ruby, I was hooked. The syntax is easy to read, and it makes writing clean, expressive code a breeze. It's not just a tool; it feels like an extension of your thoughts, making it super easy to bring your ideas to life. It's this perfect mix of power and simplicity that makes Ruby a favorite among developers who value both productivity and creativity. In "Practical Ruby 3 Programming," we'll start by exploring the basics of Ruby, like blocks, procs, and lambdas. These powerful tools help you write flexible and reusable code, making your programs efficient and easy to maintain. As we go along, you'll learn how to handle complex data changes with ease. Ruby's ecosystem is huge and active, and knowing RubyGems is key to getting the most out of it. We'll walk through finding, installing, and managing gems, so you can easily extend your apps with community-supported libraries. You'll also get hands-on experience with popular gems like Nokogiri and Faker, which'll boost your data parsing and creating realistic test scenarios.

Performance is a huge deal for any app, and I'll show you how to benchmark your Ruby programs to identify and eliminate bottlenecks. You'll learn practical techniques to measure execution speed and optimize your code, ensuring your applications run smoothly even under heavy loads. We'll also talk about packaging your Ruby apps for distribution. You'll learn how to create executable scripts and bundle your program into gems so you can share your creations with the world, no problem. We'll also dive into version control with Git, a tool that'll totally change the way you manage and work on your projects.

You'll engage with real-world examples and practical exercises that reinforce each concept throughout this book. My goal is to give you practical knowledge that you can apply right away, turning theoretical understanding into real skills. By the time we're done, you'll be super proficient in Ruby and totally confident in your skills to build, optimize, and deploy some seriously sophisticated Ruby applications. Ruby's got a special charm that makes you feel like you're accomplishing something every time you write a line of code. "Practical Ruby 3 Programming" isn't just a bunch of lessons—it's an invitation to embrace a language that makes programming enjoyable and rewarding.

Let's go on this journey together, unlocking the full potential of Ruby and transforming the way you create web applications and programs.

Content

Preface

This book gives Ruby fans the skills they need to become well-versed in Ruby and build solid applications. It starts with the basics and moves on to exploring the power of blocks, procs, and lambdas. You'll learn how these constructs make your code more flexible and reusable. As you go through it, you'll learn about enumerators, which help you streamline iteration and handle complex data transformations with ease. Then, you'll dive into the exciting world of RubyGems, where you'll learn to find, install, and manage gems like a pro. You'll get hands-on with popular gems like Nokogiri and Faker, showing how to take Ruby to the next level for tasks like parsing HTML and generating realistic test data. And you'll even learn how to create and distribute your own custom gems, so you can share your innovations with the entire Ruby community.

Performance is a big focus too, with techniques for measuring how well Ruby programs run and finding the things that slow them down. It also covers packaging Ruby applications in detail, showing how to create executables and prepare programs for seamless distribution to your users. It's all about keeping track of changes with Git, working with others, and keeping your project history neat and tidy. By the time you're done with this book, you'll have a firm grasp on Ruby and the know-how to create, optimize, and deploy cutting-edge Ruby applications. This book will take all you Ruby fanatics and transform you into proficient developers. You'll be ready to take on real-world challenges and contribute to the whole Ruby ecosystem.

In this book you will learn to:

- Get a handle on Ruby's blocks, procs, and lambdas so you can create flexible, reusable code.
- Use enumerators to quickly handle complex data transformations and iteration processes.
- Find and manage RubyGems to add more features to your apps with libraries made by the community.
- Measure performance and identify code bottlenecks with benchmarking techniques.
- Package your Ruby applications into ready-to-go executables and gems for easy distribution.
- Use Git for version control to track changes, collaborate, and keep a clean project history.
- Use popular gems like Nokogiri and Faker to improve how you parse data and generate realistic test data.
- Follow best practices for debugging, performance optimization, and dependency management for apps.

GitforGits

Prerequisites

Whether you're a beginner stepping into the world of programming or an experienced developer looking to deepen your Ruby expertise, this book is designed to meet you where you are and elevate your skills to new heights.

Codes Usage

Are you in need of some helpful code examples to assist you in your programming and documentation? Look no further! Our book offers a wealth of supplemental material, including code examples and exercises.

Not only is this book here to aid you in getting your job done, but you have our permission to use the example code in your programs and documentation. However, please note that if you are reproducing a significant portion of the code, we do require you to contact us for permission.

But don't worry, using several chunks of code from this book in your program or answering a question by citing our book and quoting example code does not require permission. But if you do choose to give credit, an attribution typically includes the title, author, publisher, and ISBN. For example, "Practical Ruby 3 Programming by Zorin Fylix".

If you are unsure whether your intended use of the code examples falls under fair use or the permissions outlined above, please do not hesitate to reach out to us at support@gitforgits.com.

We are happy to assist and clarify any concerns.

Acknowledgement

I owe a tremendous debt of gratitude to GitforGits, for their unflagging enthusiasm and wise counsel throughout the entire process of writing this book. Their knowledge and careful editing helped make sure the piece was useful for people of all reading levels and comprehension skills. In addition, I'd like to thank everyone involved in the publishing process for their efforts in making this book a reality. Their efforts, from copyediting to advertising, made the project what it is today.

Finally, I'd like to express my gratitude to everyone who has shown me unconditional love and encouragement throughout my life. Their support was crucial to the completion of this book. I appreciate your help with this endeavour and your continued interest in my career.

Chapter 1: Getting Started with Ruby 3

Chapter Overview

This chapter gives you the basics you need to get started with Ruby 3. It'll show you how to install the language environment on Linux, and we will also take a quick peek at how different package managers or official installers make things easier, so you can decide which one is best for you. By the time you are done, you'll have a working Ruby setup, ready to run code straight from your preferred terminal or command prompt.

Next, there's an interactive shell called IRB that's great for experimenting. IRB is really handy because you can experiment with syntax, do some arithmetic, and tinker with strings in real time. This hands-on tinkering helps you learn the fundamentals of Ruby without having to repeatedly create and edit files. You'll get a feel for Ruby, and that'll give you the confidence to try things out right away.

Finally, there's a section that covers writing and running your own Ruby scripts. A short code snippet that prints messages or performs simple calculations will show you the building blocks of Ruby syntax. And when you pass parameters to the scripts, it'll give you a new perspective on basic command-line operations. All this practical knowledge is a perfect foundation for tackling more ambitious projects, since everything else in the language is based on your ability to run code and see how Ruby responds.

Installing Ruby on Linux

Installing Ruby on Linux

Ruby's becoming more popular, and people are curious about why so many programmers are choosing it. If you look at community forums or GitHub repositories, you'll see that Ruby's simplicity, readability, and focus on developer happiness continue to make it popular with experienced professionals and beginners. Its emphasis on rapid prototyping, together with a strong emphasis on object-oriented paradigms, has fueled the surge of frameworks and libraries that make common tasks faster. And for those of us who are more into Linux, Ruby works seamlessly with various distributions, making installation a breeze without any of that complicated dependency drama. The documentation is really helpful, and the discussion boards are a great place to get friendly solutions to your questions. With Ruby 3 running in our main Linux setup, every demo will give you a feel for the familiar open-source environment.

Step-by-Step Installation with Package Managers

A direct way to install Ruby 3 on Ubuntu involves using built-in repositories. A typical setup might begin with an update command that fetches the latest package information. One can open a terminal, then use:

```
sudo apt-get update
sudo apt-get install ruby-full
```

There are similar commands exist for Fedora or other distributions, often using **dnf** or **yum** in place of **apt-get**. A check for version details comes afterward, using **ruby -v** to confirm that the system recognizes Ruby 3.x. It is worth noting that older versions might appear if the repositories lag behind official releases, prompting individuals to enable specialized repositories or explore alternative approaches. This whole entire procedure typically takes just a few minutes, and the result is a fully operational Ruby installation that integrates well with the Linux filesystem.

Using RVM or 'rbenv'

A more flexible option involves installing Ruby Version Manager (RVM) or rbenv. Either tool grants the freedom to toggle among different Ruby versions or gem sets on the same computer, making it ideal for projects that demand distinctive environments. A typical RVM installation might include these commands:

```
sudo apt-get update
sudo apt-get install curl g++ make
\curl -sSL https://get.rvm.io | bash -s stable --ruby=3.0
source ~/.rvm/scripts/rvm
```

The line invoking a remote script from **get.rvm.io** configures your environment, though caution is advised when executing scripts directly from the internet. Meanwhile, rbenv follows a comparable process, involving a Git clone, environment variable setup, and a plugin installation for building Ruby 3. With both methods, switching versions or installing new ones becomes quick, so teams with varied requirements often embrace these tools.

Verifying Installation

A simple verification step involves running **ruby -v** again to confirm the newly installed version. A sample code snippet helps ensure everything is in good shape. Placing the following content in a file called **hello.rb** can serve as a final check:

```
puts "Hello from Ruby 3!"
```

A run using **ruby hello.rb** prints the message on the terminal, letting you gauge whether the environment is fully configured. An opening message like that may seem modest, yet it reflects a successful setup that will anchor all future lessons. Any installation hiccups can often be traced back to missing dependencies or conflicting older packages, and referencing distribution-specific documentation can help rectify those cases. By reaching this point, the foundation is laid for more advanced techniques, providing a comfortable space to experiment with everything Ruby 3 has to offer.

Using Interactive Ruby (IRB) Shell

Introduction to IRB

IRB is great because it can turn your ideas into Ruby output right away. You can type expressions into a prompt and watch the language process each command without creating a separate file. This feature is useful for those who want to explore a method, test a snippet, or experiment with new ideas. A sense of control over immediate feedback bolsters confidence, enabling deeper engagement with Ruby's syntax and runtime behaviors. An example might include trying out string methods, such as calling **`"Hello World".downcase`**, which instantly returns **`"hello world"`**. That immediate insight feeds a spirit of exploration, pushing one to adapt, refine, or iterate on code constructs rapidly. By regularly diving into IRB, one better understands Ruby's responsive nature and accumulates practical knowledge of how everyday commands operate.

Launching IRB

A simple launch from a terminal involves typing **`irb`** or, in some distributions, using **`irb --simple-prompt`**. A short welcome message often appears, along with a prompt labeled something like **`irb(main):001:`**. From there, typed code lines execute instantly upon pressing Enter. A basic demonstration might be verifying arithmetic behaviors by typing **`10 * 3`**, which immediately shows **`30`** as the evaluation result. For more structured tests, a short loop can be entered:

```
3.times do |index|
  puts "Index: #{index}"
end
```

Each iteration then prints a line in real time. Exiting IRB involves typing **`exit`** or pressing **`Ctrl+D`**, restoring the terminal to its usual state. By tapping into IRB for quick checks and iterative exploration, one discovers an efficient way to validate assumptions or ensure certain operations produce the expected output.

Practical Demonstrations and Experimentation

An appealing aspect of IRB involves using built-in commands to learn more about specific objects. A call such as **`"hello".methods`** reveals an array of methods available on a string object. A closer look might include analyzing **`String.instance_methods(false)`** to see methods exclusive to the **`String`** class. Another approach tests conditionals or small functions without formal file structures, allowing one to quickly switch between ideas. For instance, a sample conditional in IRB might be:

```
name = "Ruby"
if name == "Ruby"
  puts "Match found!"
else
  puts "No match!"
end
```

That snippet verifies if a variable holds a specific value before giving live feedback. Frequent use of IRB thus shapes a daily habit, reinforcing Ruby's syntax while reducing the friction of saving, running, and re-editing multiple times. Even tasks like parsing small JSON strings or converting data sets become more convenient when done interactively.

A few tips that can enhance the IRB is like an arrow-key press (up or down) cycles through command history, letting one quickly modify previous lines instead of retyping them. A **`.quit`** command is another way to leave the shell if **`exit`** or **`Ctrl+D`** feels unfamiliar. Meanwhile, exploring additional libraries or attempting more advanced Ruby features in IRB remains a common approach for learning.

Basic Program Execution

An early snippet was presented previously, referencing a **`hello.rb`** example that printed a brief greeting. That approach involved storing Ruby commands inside a text file, which the Ruby interpreter reads and processes from top to bottom. With commands such as **`puts "Hello Ruby!"`** in a file, one is able to use the command line to invoke **`ruby hello.rb`**. Such an invocation triggers the interpreter to parse the file, interpret each line, and produce output. This method remains one of the core ways to develop and deliver any program built using Ruby, whether it's a short script or a more elaborate application spanning multiple files.

Creating Sample Program

An illustrative script might contain operations that gather user input, perform calculations, or manipulate text. Suppose you create a file called **`example_script.rb`** to explore a slight variation of what was done in previous segments:

```
# example_script.rb
```

```
numbers = [5, 10, 15]
sum = numbers.reduce(0) { |acc, num| acc + num }
puts "The sum of the array is #{sum}"
```

A snippet like this gives a small insight into how arrays can hold a list of numbers, and how Ruby's built-in **reduce** method sums those numbers neatly. By saving that file in the same directory as your terminal location, running **ruby example_script.rb** displays the total. Here, the convenience lies in bundling logic within a file that can be reused multiple times, committed to version control, and shared with others. One might add more lines to manipulate the array further, such as sorting or applying transformations, without retyping commands interactively.

Executing Ruby Scripts

A typical execution pattern begins with the **ruby filename.rb** approach. That direct usage spawns the Ruby interpreter, feeds it the chosen file, and exits once all statements are processed. Another alternative involves marking the file as executable on Linux by adding a "shebang" line at the top (e.g., **#!/usr/bin/env ruby**), then granting execution permission with a command like **chmod +x example_script.rb**. After that, running **./example_script.rb** from the command line yields the same result, but it saves you from typing **ruby** each time. This approach is more common in Linux environments, especially for scripts used in automation tasks. If one makes any edits to the script, simply re-running the same command displays updated results, offering a straightforward development loop for Ruby-based projects or utilities.

Passing Command-Line Arguments

An essential feature of script-based programming is the handling of arguments provided at runtime. By leveraging the **ARGV** array, Ruby exposes command-line inputs directly to your script. A minor addition to the previous example can highlight how you might greet someone by name:

```
# greet.rb
puts "Hello, #{ARGV[0]}!"
```

Calling **ruby greet.rb Alice** prints out "Hello, Alice!" The positional arguments after the script name become accessible through **ARGV** in sequential order, so **ARGV[0]** is "Alice," **ARGV[1]** is the second input, and so on. This approach extends to more advanced use cases, such as specifying file paths or toggling particular modes in your script. A short snippet:

```
# greet_info.rb
name = ARGV[0]
```

```
city = ARGV[1]
puts "Hello, #{name}. You're from #{city}, right?"
```

If you invoke **`ruby greet_info.rb Bob Seattle`**, the script references **`ARGV[0]`** as "Bob" and **`ARGV[1]`** as "Seattle," customizing the greeting accordingly. This concept can be extended to parse flags or advanced argument structures, though that typically leads to libraries like **`OptionParser`** for more sophisticated handling. A script that processes text could be paired with the standard input or piped output from other commands. Another script might rely on environment variables to configure runtime behavior without altering the code. These possibilities illustrate why many developers appreciate using Ruby for quick tasks or automation jobs. The structure is minimal, requiring just a file with **`.rb`** extension and direct instructions to run it. As projects expand, that same approach remains valid but grows to encompass more files, classes, and modules for organization.

Summary

It was pretty cool how everyone figured out they could install Ruby 3 on Linux straight up. You could see the confidence building as people got it set up with terminal commands. It was like a light bulb moment, showing that Ruby's environment could be set up in a jiffy. Everyone started recognizing package managers and official repositories, and suddenly, everyone could adapt the setup process to their own operating system without stressing out. There was a sense of satisfaction when we tested the results with some basic commands to make sure everything was running smoothly.

IRB was also cool because it let you run short code snippets right away, showing you the results as you went. This made people want to experiment more, seeing how variables, loops, and other constructs worked. It felt really free, because you could adjust code in IRB with just one command instead of editing lots of files.

Apart from that, it was also clear that running Ruby scripts meant putting commands into a file and letting the interpreter process them. This approach lets people reuse, share, and improve their logic across different runs. These steps, taken together, showed a basic workflow where installing the language, practicing in IRB, and running scripts contributed to a flexible foundation for future growth.

Chapter 2: Up and Running with Ruby Syntax

Chapter Overview

Exploring this new chapter will give you a deeper understanding of Ruby's core language features and how they interact with fundamental elements. When you take a closer look at how literals work, it becomes clearer how text, numbers, and symbols behave in Ruby. You'll see the subtle details of different data representations that show up in everyday scripts. Then, we'll dive into variables and constants, where we'll see how names reflect their scope and purpose. This helps you figure out how to strike a balance between making code easy to read and keeping it maintainable. It also helps you tell the difference between temporary storage and values that don't change.

Another thing that comes up is the idea of keyword arguments and how handy default values are in methods. If you use these features, you can write function calls that make it clear what you mean while also helping to avoid accidentally passing parameters in the wrong order. When every argument has a name, the code is clearer, which helps teams and individuals understand what the method does. On top of that, default values let methods deal with missing parameters without needing extra conditionals. When you put all this together, it helps you really understand the language, building on lessons about how you structure data and how it flows through Ruby's flexible syntax.

Working with Literals

Overview of Numeric Literals

There's a lot to learn from exploring numeric literals in Ruby. You can see how integers, floats, and other numeric formats can appear without a bunch of syntax. A straightforward integer might be **`42`**, while a floating-point number could be **`3.14`**. An individual can create a larger integer without any special markup, since Ruby natively supports big integers. A typical scenario might involve performing arithmetic directly on these values, as in **`x = 42 + 10`**, and Ruby handles the result gracefully. A focus on underscores in large numbers, such as **`1_000_000`**, demonstrates that readability takes precedence while the numeric value remains unaffected. One can also define hexadecimal or octal numbers, like **`0xFF`** or **`0o377`**, each recognized by the Ruby interpreter. By acknowledging these patterns, you gain insight into how Ruby parses numbers behind the scenes, ultimately granting freedom to represent values needed in calculations or data processing tasks. Even negative numbers work in the same manner, expressed as **`-5`**, confirming that sign prefixes don't break the literal form. A detail worth noting is that floating-point calculations occasionally introduce rounding quirks, a common occurrence in many languages. This helps highlight that numeric literals come in various shapes, ensuring that your scripts can store, manipulate, and display values spanning typical day-to-day operations or more advanced numeric routines.

Strings

Another aspect of Ruby's literal usage emerges with strings, which offer multiple ways to embed text. A single-quoted string might be **'Hello World'**, where the text remains mostly verbatim, treating backslashes and certain escape characters as standard text. A double-quoted string, like **"Hello\nWorld"**, allows special escape sequences to transform into actual newlines or tab characters. An enthusiastic scripter might also take advantage of string interpolation by wrapping expressions in **#{}**, so **"The sum is #{x + y}"** merges the result of **x + y** directly within the text. A triple-quoted approach can surface through here-documents, providing an option to embed lengthy text blocks in a more readable format.

For example, something like:

```
message = <<~TEXT
  This is a multi-line string
  that preserves formatting
  in a tidy way.
TEXT
```

captures large textual content without forcing extraneous concatenations or plus signs. This style demonstrates how Ruby encourages flexible representation of textual data, helping you write clearer code and ensuring that plain words or dynamic content can merge conveniently. A thorough handle on these variations supports most text-handling tasks, whether you are producing logs, generating user-visible messages, or analyzing incoming textual data.

Symbols

A distinct feature in Ruby is the Symbol literal, marked by a leading colon, such as **:example**. Symbols are recognized as immutable identifiers, serving as efficient placeholders for labeling things like hash keys or method names without incurring the overhead typical of repeatedly duplicated strings. By referencing **:id** or **:status**, one is effectively assigning a stable, memory-friendly label that remains the same object throughout the program. A scenario might look like **user = { name: "Alice", age: 30, status: :active }**, in which case **:active** stands as a symbol in that hash. The choice between strings and symbols hinges on usage context: a symbol tends to remain consistent and is often used for identifiers, while a string is better when textual manipulation is required. The concept of a symbol encourages a pattern in which you rely on small placeholders for referencing categories, states, or settings without tying them to their string representation each time. Although some developers prefer string keys out of habit, symbols remain a central part of Ruby's approach to labeling and referencing consistent values across the application's flow.

Boolean Values

Those seeking a direct approach to expressing truth values in Ruby encounter **true** and **false** as the built-in Boolean literals, reflecting yes-or-no states in conditionals or logic gates. Although some languages might include multiple truthy or falsey forms, Ruby narrows it down so that anything besides **false** or **nil** is considered true in conditional checks.

For example, by writing a snippet like:

```
value = true

if value

  puts "Value is true!"

else

  puts "Value is false!"

end
```

one observes that the block under the **if** statement executes whenever **value** is anything except **false** or **nil**. This clarity explains how Ruby's conditionals operate, ensuring minimal confusion when strings, numbers, or objects become tested. The presence of these Boolean literals emphasizes the importance of clarity in logic. A check for **value.nil?** is another vital approach to detect when something is undefined, since Ruby interprets **nil** as the absence of a valid object. By preserving a straightforward approach to Boolean checks, the language keeps the code expressive without inundating it with extraneous forms of falsehood or truth.

Sample Program: Numeric, String, Symbol, and Boolean Literals all together

Now, let us consider something like:

```
# literals_demo.rb

number = 100

temperature = 37.5

greeting = "Hello, Ruby!"

status_symbol = :active

is_running = true

puts "Number: #{number}"

puts "Temperature: #{temperature}"
```

```
puts "Greeting: #{greeting}"
puts "Status Symbol: #{status_symbol}"
puts "Is Running? #{is_running}"
if is_running
  puts "Process has started..."
else
  puts "Process not active."
end
# Symbol usage in a hash:
info = { user_name: "Alice", user_status: status_symbol }
puts "User Name: #{info[:user_name]}, User Status:
#{info[:user_status]}"
```

A script like this prints out the assigned numeric and string values, reveals the symbol usage in a status context, and checks the Boolean to decide which message to display. By storing **:active** in **status_symbol** and referencing it in the **info** hash, one sees how symbols help label categories or states. Notice that double-quoted strings allow interpolation with **#{}**, so we can easily display variable data. By running this script with **ruby literals_demo.rb**, you witness how these literal types unify to convey everything from numeric data to textual messages, while relying on Boolean control and symbol-based identification.

Variables and Constants

Differentiating Variables and Naming Conventions

To get a handle on how Ruby handles variables, you'll first need to know that local variables tend to start with a lowercase letter or an underscore. A name like **user_name** or **_tempValue** represents a place to store data that can change over time. One might see variables assigned multiple times to capture shifting states, such as **temperature = 20.0**, then **temperature = 21.5** a bit later. That adjustment reflects the flexible nature of local variables, which hold onto whatever you assign to them. In a file-scoped or method-scoped context, these variables are accessible only within that scope, preventing accidental interference from other parts of the application. By contrast, a global variable would start with **$**, though many developers avoid them for clarity and modular design. A class variable, beginning with **@@**, holds data shared across all instances of a class, while instance variables use an **@** prefix, storing values that belong to a specific object. Those naming distinctions steer how data is shared, making it easier to predict whether any piece of code might adjust to a certain state.

Let us look at our previous example on **literals_demo.rb**, and expand further to illustrate how new variables fit into that code. Let us say that you track an environment name or user role that changes based on context.

Now here, the snippet would look like:

```
environment = "development"
role = :admin
puts "Current environment: #{environment}"
puts "User role: #{role}"
environment = "production"
role = :guest
puts "Environment updated to: #{environment}"
puts "User role changed to: #{role}"
```

The above program highlights how local variables shift seamlessly. The script merges these local variables with the previously explored numeric, string, symbol, and boolean literals. When you put them together, you'll see that each line updates or displays data. This shows that variables let your script respond to inputs or evolving states without having to rewrite entire logic blocks. That sense of adaptability is really important for real-world applications, where different paths might be taken depending on variable values.

Understanding Constants

If you take a look at the constants, you'll see that the names all start with an uppercase letter. A typical example might be **MAX_ATTEMPTS = 3**, set near the top of a file to indicate that this value must remain static throughout execution. Ruby allows changes to constants, but it will produce a warning when you reassign them, signaling that doing so goes against the intention of naming something a constant. A scenario might be storing a version number or the name of an application in a constant to ensure that other parts of the code do not unintentionally overwrite it.

If we check the previous program, we might be able to reveal how constants interact with variables:

```
MAX_USERS = 5
current_users = 2
puts "Maximum allowed: #{MAX_USERS}"
```

```
puts "Currently online: #{current_users}"
current_users += 1
puts "Another user joined. New total: #{current_users}"
```

A piece of code like this clarifies that **MAX_USERS** remains stable, while **current_users** shifts as new sign-ins occur. If a developer attempts to change **MAX_USERS** later, Ruby may complain about the constant reassignment. That behavior offers a gentle nudge to keep constant usage consistent, preventing accidental modifications that might disrupt the program's internal assumptions. It also fosters a clear boundary between what is intended to be permanent (or at least stable) and what the script can manipulate freely.

Integrating Variables and Constants

A natural continuation of **literals_demo.rb** lets you expand by adding constants for any essential fixed values. Suppose the application tracks a maximum threshold for temperature or a default user status:

```
# literals_demo.rb
MAX_TEMPERATURE = 38.0
DEFAULT_STATUS = :inactive
number = 100
temperature = 37.5
greeting = "Hello, Ruby!"
status_symbol = :active
is_running = true
environment = "development"
role = :admin
puts "Number: #{number}"
puts "Temperature: #{temperature}"
puts "Greeting: #{greeting}"
puts "Status Symbol: #{status_symbol}"
puts "Is Running? #{is_running}"
puts "Environment: #{environment}, Role: #{role}"
puts "Maximum Temperature: #{MAX_TEMPERATURE}"
```

```
puts "Default Status: #{DEFAULT_STATUS}"
```

A file like this shows variables and constants working side by side. Notice that constants adopt uppercase naming, possibly with underscores, while local variables use lowercase. If you decided to override **MAX_TEMPERATURE**, Ruby would print a warning, acknowledging that constants are not truly immutable but should be treated as such. By running **ruby literals_demo.rb** again, output now includes the new constants among the standard variables. Through experimentation, you can see precisely how variables enable immediate changes in flow or data, while constants are left untouched. This pattern becomes more significant as scripts expand, because it delineates which values remain stable even when developers refactor or enhance features.

Keyword Arguments and Default Values

Introducing Keyword Arguments

Ruby's flexibility is really important, and it shows up in how you use keyword arguments. Instead of method parameters being referred to by their position in the code, they're referenced by name.

Given below is an example that shows clarity in writing:

```
def user_info(name:, age:, status:)
  puts "Name: #{name}"
  puts "Age: #{age}"
  puts "Status: #{status}"
end
user_info(name: "Alice", age: 30, status: :active)
```

A method call with labeled parameters stands out as self-describing, reducing confusion about the order in which arguments should appear. An advantage surfaces when many parameters exist, because each argument is clarified by a name. A next step might involve optional arguments, such as **status:** being left out if it's not relevant to that invocation. By adopting this named format, code often reads like a sentence that describes exactly what is being passed. That clear way of doing things is a real help when putting together a bunch of data points, and it makes sure you don't accidentally put the wrong stuff in. Another thing to note is how Ruby can make sure that certain keywords are there and that you don't skip over important arguments without saying so. So, every time you call a function that works with data, it's clear and consistent, which is just what Ruby likes for its data calls.

Using Default Values in Methods

A second dimension of convenience arrives through default values, which let you omit a parameter when calling a method. Given below is a quick syntax example which would appear as:

```
def greet_user(name: "Guest", greeting: "Hello")
  puts "#{greeting}, #{name}!"
end
greet_user
greet_user(name: "Bob")
greet_user(greeting: "Hi", name: "Carol")
```

The above snippet displays how the method **`greet_user`** can assume "Guest" and "Hello" if neither argument is explicitly supplied. A design like this spares you from writing multiple versions of the same method or adding conditionals every time you handle missing inputs. It also fosters a coding style that leads to fewer lines overall. A method that handles an optional parameter such as **`status: :inactive`** might be part of a workflow that toggles certain features only when a user is active. The outcome is a more condensed way to handle input that might or might not surface each time your method is invoked.

Now, let us look at the integration of keyword arguments and default values:

```
# literals_demo.rb
MAX_TEMPERATURE = 38.0
DEFAULT_STATUS = :inactive
def show_system_info(environment: "development", role: :guest,
temperature: 36.5, status: DEFAULT_STATUS)
  puts "Environment: #{environment}"
  puts "Role: #{role}"
  puts "Current Temperature: #{temperature}"
  puts "Status: #{status}"
end
number = 100
temperature = 37.5
greeting = "Hello, Ruby!"
```

```
status_symbol = :active
is_running = true
# Call method with some arguments omitted
show_system_info
puts "-----"
# Call method with explicit parameters
show_system_info(environment: "production", role: :admin,
temperature: temperature, status: status_symbol)
puts "-----"
```

Here, a method **show_system_info** demonstrates how optional parameters align with the content used in earlier topics. Each named parameter is assigned a sensible default, so calling **show_system_info** with no arguments yields an environment of "development" and a role of **:guest**, along with a temperature of 36.5 and the default status. A second call provides explicit arguments to override those defaults, revealing how easily the method adapts to context. By weaving this concept into the existing script, one notices that default values reduce the need to write conditional statements for missing arguments. It encourages reusability, letting you experiment with each parameter independently. A logical extension might involve including a maximum temperature check, ensuring that if the provided temperature exceeds **MAX_TEMPERATURE**, a warning is displayed. This approach remains easy to implement, relying on the method's flexible argument structure. Each piece of data, from environment to role, can be named clearly in any method call, ensuring others who read the code know precisely what each argument represents.

Summary

So, we took a deep dive into how Ruby handles literal forms like numbers, strings, symbols, and boolean values. We figured out that each type has its own purpose. With strings, you can manipulate text flexibly, and symbols are efficient identifiers for data structures. We also used arithmetic expressions and interpolation techniques in our daily scripting tasks to keep the code concise and readable. Everyone knew that booleans and nil influenced conditions in a predictable way, reducing confusion when deciding which paths to execute.Another focus was on the role of variables and constants within programs.Assignments were observed to shift data states or maintain stable references through uppercase naming, signaling values that resisted frequent updates.By distinguishing local, instance, and global variables, new possibilities emerged for structuring code that precisely handled information.

Then, we turned our attention to keyword arguments and default values, which made function calls clearer. These methods focused on explicit naming and optional parameters, making usage simpler for developers and encouraging stronger intent in method definitions. Each component—literals, variables, and keywords—provided a deeper appreciation for Ruby's approach to expressive and accessible syntax. It also made it so that developers had more control over how data flowed, which made them feel more confident about Ruby's ability to adapt.

Chapter 3: Exploring Control Flow and Blocks

Chapter Overview

In this chapter, we focus on how Ruby controls the flow of a program and orchestrates repetitive operations. We look into conditionals such as **if**, **elsif**, and **case** revealing the language's ability to decide among multiple paths based on your data or variables. We then look into loops like **while** and **until**, each of them are capable of cycling through blocks of code until a condition changes. By practicing these techniques, we build a foundational skill set for directing logic, halting sequences, or skipping certain iterations at the right moment. An additional emphasis on blocks highlights how Ruby allows snippets of code to be treated as objects, letting you hand them off to methods like **each** or **map**.

Each of these topics lead directly to numbered parameters to handle block arguments. Next, a quick look at **_1**, **_2**, and more shows how code becomes leaner when referencing multiple inputs. The synergy between loops and blocks paves the way for a more expressive style, letting you focus on outcomes rather than boilerplate. With all these, you can discover how Ruby's syntax encourages clarity and directness, even when dealing with branching paths and repeated tasks.

Conditionals and Loops

'if' Statements

An if statement is often the first structure people reach for when controlling program flow in Ruby. A condition like **if temperature > 37** can decide which branch of code runs, ensuring that only relevant lines execute under certain circumstances.

Let us look at the following code:

```
# conditionals_demo.rb
temperature = 37.5
if temperature > 37
  puts "Temperature is above normal."
else
  puts "Temperature is within normal range."
end
```

A condition like **if temperature > 37** checks the boolean result, and if it's true, Ruby runs the enclosed code. If not, the else block fires. That approach is easy to read, letting you tailor logic around an expression that might evaluate to either true or false. Another extension could include an **elsif** section if more than two possible paths exist. For instance:

```
if temperature > 39
  puts "Fever alert!"
elsif temperature > 37
  puts "Slightly elevated."
else
  puts "All good!"
end
```

Each condition is tested in sequence, stopping once a match is found.

'case' Structure

A more streamlined way to handle multiple distinct values appears through case statements. A snippet in the same **conditionals_demo.rb** might look like:

```
status = :active
case status
when :active
  puts "User is active."
when :inactive
  puts "User is inactive."
when :banned
  puts "User access blocked."
else
  puts "Unknown status."
end
```

A direct mapping of possible states to outcomes is shown, and Ruby automatically compares **status** with each when condition. A single else clause captures anything that doesn't match the listed values. This method can be clearer when dealing with multiple symbols or constants, making the program easy to follow. A pattern emerges where data such as **:admin** or **:guest** can be matched to specific instructions. If more detailed checks are needed, the when clauses can incorporate ranges or expressions, such as **when 1..5**, or even call methods if you are comfortable passing logic into the when line. By focusing on neat groupings, you keep code structured and avoid sprawling if-elsif blocks.

'while' Loops

A while loop iterates as long as a condition remains true. It works nicely when a definite exit path is known or if you are reacting to variables in real time. Suppose you extend the script with:

```
counter = 0
while counter < 3
  puts "Counter at #{counter}"
  counter += 1
end
puts "Loop finished!"
```

The condition **counter < 3** is checked before each iteration, so once counter hits 3, Ruby skips the loop. That style is practical for repeated tasks that require constant verification of state, such as listening for user input or collecting sensor data. An alternative is **until**, which loops until a condition becomes true, flipping the logic around. If a scenario demands continuing until a variable hits a threshold, that approach can read more naturally. The choice between while and until relies on which version is clearer for the scenario at hand. Either loop can incorporate break statements to stop early or next statements to skip to the next iteration.

Implementing 'for' Loops

A for loop provides a simpler iteration pattern for sequences. Ruby programmers sometimes prefer iterators like **each**, but for loops remain an option. A snippet might appear as:

```
for i in 1..3
  puts "Value of i is #{i}"
end
```

This code prints numbers from 1 to 3 inclusive, repeating the block for each integer. A half-open range (1...3) excludes the end, so it would iterate for 1 and 2 only. Although for loops are less common in idiomatic Ruby (where enumerators and blocks dominate), they still appear in some scripts or when clarity demands a typical loop structure. For short tasks, a for loop can be straightforward, especially if you are used to loops from other languages. However, Ruby's collection methods (**each**, **map**, **select**) often yield more concise solutions. Still, the for loop remains a valid choice for scanning through numeric ranges or enumerating items in an array.

Sample Program: Integrating Conditionals and Loops

A unified example could appear by enhancing the existing code from earlier chapters. Consider a file that merges variables, constants, and a few condition checks:

```
MAX_COUNT = 4
def analyze_temperature(temp)
  if temp > 39
    puts "High fever detected."
  elsif temp > 37
    puts "Slightly elevated temperature."
  else
    puts "Temperature is normal."
  end
end
for i in 0...MAX_COUNT
  current_temp = 37.0 + i
  puts "Reading #{i}: #{current_temp}"
  analyze_temperature(current_temp)
end
```

This script loops from **0** up to **MAX_COUNT - 1** using a half-open range, generating a temperature reading each time. The method **analyze_temperature** uses a chain of if conditions to decide which message to display. A synergy occurs: the for loop provides the repeated logic, while the if/elsif structure determines which statement is printed. This interplay demonstrates real-world patterns where code repeatedly checks values and then interprets them, all within a concise framework.

Blocks and Iterators

An earlier mention highlighted that Ruby blocks are chunks of code enclosed in braces (**{}**) or do/end pairs, and they can be passed around as method arguments. A brief reminder: these blocks capture context and variables, often simplifying repeated operations on collections. A typical scenario might involve arrays or hashes, where a block processes each item or key-value pair. By exploring a few examples, it becomes clearer how these iterators replace verbose looping constructs, improving code readability.

'each' Method

A popular iterator in Ruby is **each**, commonly used with arrays or hashes. An array example might appear as follows:

```
numbers = [1, 2, 3, 4]
numbers.each do |num|
  puts "Number: #{num}"
end
```

Every element in **numbers** is passed to the block, where **num** references the current item. That approach condenses a typical for or while loop into a simpler expression. For a hash, you might write something like:

```
user = { name: "Alice", role: :admin }
user.each do |key, value|
  puts "#{key} => #{value}"
end
```

That snippet displays each pair in the hash. By aligning the block parameters with the collection's structure, Ruby ensures that your code remains concise. An iteration over larger data sets becomes straightforward, particularly when combined with conditional checks or transformations inside the block.

Transforming Data with 'map'

Another iterator, **map**, processes each item in a collection, applies a block, and returns a new array based on the result. An example might appear as:

```
numbers = [1, 2, 3, 4]
squares = numbers.map do |num|
  num * num
end
puts squares.inspect
```

The output becomes **[1, 4, 9, 16]**, revealing that each element was squared. A difference from **each** is that **map** produces a transformed array without altering the original, unless you use **map!** to apply changes in place. One might rely on **map** to convert strings to uppercase, reformat data for display, or parse numeric values from text. By focusing on a one-line transformation, code remains easier to follow. A practice that pairs well with **map** is chaining multiple calls, such as chaining **select**, **map**, and so forth, although that pattern can appear more frequently when exploring enumerators in detail. Regardless, **map** remains a workhorse for tasks that require altering collection contents in a single pass.

Additional Iterator Methods

Enumerables in Ruby pack numerous iterators beyond **each** and **map**. A few notable examples include:

- **select**: Filters a collection based on a condition, returning elements for which the block evaluates to true.
- **reject**: Inverse of **select**, discarding elements that match the block condition.
- **reduce** (also known as **inject**): Accumulates a result by applying the block to each element alongside a running total.
- **each_with_index**: Provides both item and index to the block, handy when you need positional context.

See the following a quick sample implementation:

```
numbers = [1, 2, 3, 4, 5]
even_numbers = numbers.select { |n| n.even? }
sum_of_all = numbers.reduce(0) { |acc, n| acc + n }
puts "Even numbers: #{even_numbers.inspect}"
puts "Sum of numbers: #{sum_of_all}"
```

This snippet demonstrates how easily one can filter out even values and compute a sum in just a few lines. By gradually practicing each of these iterator methods, patterns form around how to accomplish common tasks with minimal code.

Sample Program: Integrating Iterators

Let us extend our existing program wherein the file **conditionals_demo.rb** or a new file contains:

```
def analyze_temperatures(temps)
  temps.each do |temp|
    if temp > 39
      puts "#{temp} -> High fever detected."
    elsif temp > 37
```

```
      puts "#{temp} -> Slightly elevated."
    else
      puts "#{temp} -> Normal temperature."
    end
  end
end
readings = [36.5, 37.2, 38.5, 39.1, 40.0]
analyze_temperatures(readings)
puts "-----"
mapped_readings = readings.map { |r| r.round }
puts "Rounded Readings: #{mapped_readings.inspect}"
```

A new method, **analyze_temperatures**, leverages **each** loop to classify multiple temperature values. This chunk goes beyond a single numeric check, scanning a series of results in a simple block. Another line uses a **map** to produce a fresh list of rounded temperatures, demonstrating how that transformation can occur without additional loops. Such usage cements the idea that a few lines of Ruby handle iteration neatly, blending conditions with block operations.

Numbered Parameters in Blocks

Introducing Numbered Parameters

In Ruby, knowing about numbered parameters can really streamline your blocks. A typical block might define parameters between vertical bars, such as **|item|**, but with numbered parameters, Ruby automatically assigns names like **_1** and **_2** for the first and second arguments. This feature eliminates the need to type custom parameter names when code clarity allows a more compact approach. By referencing **_1**, one can process the first argument directly. Multiple arguments follow suit, enabling **_2** for the second, **_3** for the third, and so on. This style can feel natural when the block requires minimal interaction with arguments or if a quick filter or transform is all that's needed.

For example, following is the code snippet:

```
[1, 2, 3].each { puts _1 }
```

can become shorter than the traditional **|num|** version. Though optional, some developers prefer the explicit naming, especially in more complex code. Still, the new approach can add brevity when clarity remains intact.

Basic Usage with Arrays and Hashes

A block using numbered parameters remains identical in logic to one that defines named parameters. For arrays, each element is assigned to **_1** whenever the block runs, so a call like:

```
fruits = ["apple", "banana", "cherry"]
fruits.each { puts "Fruit: #{_1}" }
```

prints each item. For a hash, a block typically sees the key and value, so:

```
user = { name: "Alice", status: :active }
user.each { puts "Key: #{_1}, Value: #{_2}" }
```

A structure like that shortens typical syntax from something like **|k, v|** to **_1** and **_2**, reducing keystrokes while retaining clarity. It remains essential to confirm that code reviewers and collaborators find numbered parameters legible. When referencing multiple arguments, the underscore plus number pattern can help keep track of which item is in focus. However, if the block grows more complex, descriptive names might be preferable. In smaller methods or succinct transformations, numbered parameters shine by emphasizing the data flow without introducing new variable names.

Sample Program

When we're talking about adding this feature to an existing script, the way to go is data processing. Suppose an array of temperature readings needs classification and printing. An example might be:

```
readings = [36.5, 37.2, 38.5, 39.1, 40.0]
readings.each do
  if _1 > 39
    puts "#{_1} -> High fever detected."
  elsif _1 > 37
    puts "#{_1} -> Slightly elevated."
  else
    puts "#{_1} -> Normal temperature."
  end
end
```

That approach demonstrates how **_1** references each temperature as the block iterates. The condition checks remain identical to what you might write with a named parameter. Another usage might be with **map**:

```
rounded_readings = readings.map { _1.round }

puts "Rounded Readings: #{rounded_readings.inspect}"
```

The **_1** placeholder again indicates the single argument arriving to the block. If one needed the index, the enumerator method could be changed to something like **each_with_index { puts "#{_1}, Index: #{_2}" }**, though remember that enumerator definitions also matter for how arguments are passed. By experimenting with this pattern, you see how it fosters quick, concise transformations or checks without devoting extra space to naming block parameters.

Integrating Numbered Parameters with Existing Methods

A natural place to integrate these parameters is within the methods and loops from earlier examples. Let us take our previous example that inspects temperature readings, then use **select** to isolate only those above a certain threshold:

```
def filter_above_threshold(values, threshold)

  values.select { _1 > threshold }

end

hot_readings = filter_above_threshold(readings, 38)

hot_readings.each { puts "Hot reading: #{_1}" }
```

This approach confirms that Ruby allows **_1** to be used inside a method's block as well, reducing the block syntax to its essentials. Another scenario might revolve around calling **reduce** to sum up numeric data.

For instance:

```
total_sum = readings.reduce(0) { _1 + _2 }

puts "Total of all readings: #{total_sum}"
```

Here, **_1** represents the accumulated value, and **_2** is the current array element, effectively removing the need to name them as `|acc, num|`. This concise notation benefits scripts with frequent small transformations or checks, letting the logic stand out without repetitive parameter definitions. Despite these advantages, there is still a trade-off: a block with many references to **_1**, **_2**, or **_3** might be less self-explanatory for future viewers of the code. Choosing descriptive names can improve clarity when the block's purpose is less obvious. However, for short loops or straightforward transformations, numbered parameters capture a direct style that lines up with Ruby's push toward readability and minimal syntax overhead. By selectively integrating this feature, you can refine your approach to block-based iterations, ensuring that the code remains both succinct and easy to follow.

Summary

We took a look at how Ruby handled conditionals, loops, and blocks, and it opened up new possibilities for structuring program logic. We found that conditionals like if and case offered natural ways to branch code, while loops such as while and for allowed repeating segments to run until a change occurred in variables or conditions. And when you put these together, it gets easier to build interactive sequences, often doing checks or collecting data in a concise way.

Then, blocks added a feeling of fluidity to the code, enabling seamless processing of items. They also introduced numbered parameters to make argument handling more compact by eliminating the need for named variables. Developers could just reference _1 or _2 within blocks, which reduced boilerplate in straightforward transformations. When we put all these features together, it became clear that Ruby's syntax makes code that reads more like natural instructions than a bunch of rigid statements. All these tools together laid the groundwork for writing scripts that respond quickly to changing values and process collections without a hitch, resulting in a final outcome that's simple and clear.

Chapter 4: Handling Errors Gracefully

Chapter Overview

This chapter zeroed in on how Ruby programs dealt with errors and unexpected situations, showing ways to raise and handle exceptions when things didn't go as planned. It also highlighted Ruby's approach to creating custom errors using the raise keyword, which helps developers clearly communicate what went wrong. This approach keeps the application running smoothly and lets you deal with issues like invalid data or failed file operations in a graceful way.

There was also this idea that you could have a cleanup process that'd keep going even if there's an error, and some people figured out that you can have logic to try again without restarting the whole thing. Then, there was this whole thing about "catch-throw patterns," which basically let you exit in a controlled way, even in complex loops or in really nested methods. This concept is similar to using labels, where throwing an error effectively redirects the flow from a deeply nested part to a more encompassing one that has established the catch.

By using these techniques together, we realized that we no longer had to worry about unexpected scenarios derailing our program, and that we could add more advanced control structures into our daily coding without much trouble. This new way of thinking about error handling and flow control made our Ruby applications stronger and more reliable.

Raising and Rescuing Exceptions

An unexpected file outage, a network glitch, or an invalid input can easily derail a Ruby script if not handled properly. A method might return an error, or a library call might fail in unpredictable ways. By learning to raise exceptions, developers signal when a program meets situations it cannot proceed with, pausing regular flow to highlight the issue. A rescue block catches that exception and prevents the entire application from terminating abruptly. This arrangement benefits those building more complex solutions, where multiple components interact and one malfunction could cause a chain reaction. A raised exception effectively says, "Stop here, handle what went wrong, and decide whether to proceed." That clarity stands at the core of Ruby's error-handling philosophy. Instead of ignoring issues, one is encouraged to explicitly mark them, supporting stable code that communicates its needs.

Using 'raise' and 'rescue'

A straightforward approach begins with intentionally raising an exception to flag a problem. For instance, one might write the **`raise "File not found"`** if an expected file is missing. That raised message halts normal flow and looks for a rescue block that can manage the situation.

Following is a simple pattern that appears as:

```
begin
  # Code that might fail
```

```
  data = File.read("missing_file.txt")
  puts data
rescue => e
  puts "Error encountered: #{e.message}"
end
```

Here, the **begin** ... **rescue** construct protects the code inside, catching any exception in **e** when something goes awry. This pattern allows for partial recovery, alternate flow, or useful logging steps that inform administrators or logs about what went wrong. A single rescue can also catch multiple error classes by checking the type of exception. For file-related concerns, something like **rescue Errno::ENOENT** specifically catches "No such file or directory" errors, letting the developer act accordingly. By scoping rescue blocks wisely, a program remains robust and avoids halting when minor issues crop up.

Customizing Exception Classes

A deeper approach emerges when you define custom exceptions to handle domain-specific concerns. An example involves creating a class that inherits from **StandardError**:

```
class TemperatureError < StandardError; end
def measure_temperature(temp)
  raise TemperatureError, "Invalid reading!" if temp < -50 ||
temp > 100
  # proceed with normal logic
  puts "Temperature recorded: #{temp}"
end
```

By raising **TemperatureError** instead of a generic exception, the code clarifies that an abnormal temperature reading occurred. A rescue block can specifically catch **TemperatureError**, ignoring other unrelated exceptions. Such a technique refines error handling, especially in larger systems where multiple components generate different kinds of exceptions. Distinguishing file system errors from custom domain issues becomes simpler if each scenario uses a specialized class. This approach reduces confusion among collaborators, ensuring that everyone knows precisely which errors might arise and how they should be addressed. By adopting custom classes, the code base grows more maintainable over time.

Sample Program: Resilient Error Handling

Let us look at a sample program that ties these ideas together. It might appear in a file called **errors_demo.rb**:

```
# errors_demo.rb
class TemperatureError < StandardError; end
def analyze_temperature(temp)
  raise TemperatureError, "Reading too high!" if temp > 39
  puts "Temperature is normal or slightly elevated: #{temp}"
end
begin
  puts "Attempting to analyze temperature."
  reading = 40
  analyze_temperature(reading)
  puts "All good with the reading."
rescue TemperatureError => e
  puts "Caught a temperature problem: #{e.message}"
rescue => e
  puts "Caught a general problem: #{e.message}"
ensure
  puts "Cleaning up after temperature analysis."
end
puts "Program continues..."
```

A call to **analyze_temperature** raises a **TemperatureError** for a reading above 39, which is then rescued specifically in **rescue TemperatureError => e**. The code prints a warning about "Reading too high!" rather than crashing. Meanwhile, a second rescue block catches any other exception, adding a safety net for unexpected issues. An **ensure** line runs regardless of success or failure, logging the action taken to finalize the process. This strategy gives an app both clarity and resilience, ensuring that errors become manageable signals rather than catastrophic halts.

Ensure and Retry Blocks

Ensure for Cleanup

The **ensure** keyword in Ruby helps organize final actions that must occur whether an exception is raised or not. This mechanism often appears in scripts that open files, manage database connections, or handle any resource that needs explicit closure. The **begin** and **rescue** blocks capture errors, yet they do not always guarantee that a resource is freed when an exception happens midway through an operation. By placing cleanup code in an **ensure** block, the script prevents leaks or orphaned resources. Whether the process encounters an error or runs to completion, everything inside **ensure** will execute. This approach promotes a clear separation between core logic and the mandatory steps that finalize or reset the environment.

Implementing Retry Mechanism

The **retry** keyword offers a structured way to reattempt an operation from inside a **rescue** block. Situations involving transient errors—like intermittent file unavailability or brief network outages—often benefit from retry logic, especially when a few seconds' wait might solve the problem. Instead of throwing an error or terminating the entire process, the script can pause, increment a counter, and try again.

Following is a quick example that combines both **ensure** and **retry**:

```
require 'time'
def read_file_with_retry(filename, max_attempts = 3)
  attempts = 0
  begin
    attempts += 1
    puts "Attempt #{attempts}: Reading file: #{filename}"
    content = File.read(filename)
    puts "File content:\n#{content}"
  rescue Errno::ENOENT => e
    puts "File not found: #{e.message}"
    if attempts < max_attempts
      puts "Waiting before retry..."
      sleep 2
      retry
    else
```

```
      puts "Reached maximum attempts. Cannot read file."
    end
  ensure
    puts "Ensuring cleanup tasks, if any were required."
  end
end
read_file_with_retry("non_existent.txt", 2)
```

The **begin** block executes the file read, and **rescue** captures the error if the file does not exist. The code checks the attempt count, waits briefly if more tries remain, and then calls **retry** to start from the top of the **begin** block. Once the attempts are exhausted, or if the file is found, program flow continues normally. The **ensure** section always runs afterward, making it clear where cleanup or finishing tasks belong. By balancing these features—robust error handling, cleanup guarantees, and selective retry logic—Ruby offers a reliable framework for dealing with many real-world uncertainties.

Catch and Throw for Non-Local Exits

Understanding 'Catch' and 'Throw'

When code pathways grow complex, a strategy might be desired that interrupts execution from deep inside nested loops or methods and jumps to a designated place higher up. Ruby's catch and throw pair accomplishes this without treating the jump as an error event. Instead, a catch block establishes a label, and throw sends execution out of the nested code back to that label. This approach can help whenever standard returns or breaks prove insufficient, or when a loop sits inside multiple layers of logic that must terminate early under special conditions. There's a benefit here for programs involving large data sets or intricate pipelines, where skipping directly to the end of a routine can save resources and keep code legible.

Using Non-Local Exits

With catch and throw, non-local exits become structured. The catch label appears in a method or block that wraps an entire operation. If a specific circumstance arises within a nested loop or sub-method, a throw statement can redirect flow back to the catch. One might see it as a carefully placed "go to" that coexists with Ruby's block-based design. This pattern helps reduce complexity when normal breaks would require additional flags or complicated condition checks in multiple places. But here, try to be mindful that overusing catch and throw can obscure how code flows, so employing it judiciously maintains clarity while reaping the benefits of a rapid exit mechanism.

Sample Program

Now let us think of a method that inspects different user records stored in nested arrays. If a "banned" user is found, the script should abort scanning immediately and jump to a higher-level routine. For such a situation, the code snippet might look like this:

```
def inspect_users(users)
  catch(:banned_found) do
    users.each do |group|
      group.each do |user|
        if user[:status] == :banned
          puts "Encountered a banned user: #{user[:name]}"
          throw(:banned_found)
        else
          puts "User ok: #{user[:name]}"
        end
      end
    end
    puts "No banned users encountered."
  end
  puts "Inspection concluded."
end
groups_data = [
  [{name: "Alice", status: :active}, {name: "Bob", status:
:banned}],
  [{name: "Carol", status: :active}, {name: "Dave", status:
:active}]
]
inspect_users(groups_data)
```

The **catch(:banned_found)** label stands at the top. If a banned user appears, the throw quickly ends scanning, jumping right past any remaining loops. No exception is raised; the procedure simply halts in a deliberate manner. That technique avoids nested break statements or additional conditions needed in deeper loops. If the entire loop finishes without encountering a banned user, the code logs that no banned user was found.

So here, because this pattern occupies a niche role, some prefer standard break statements or returns for simpler loops. However, when multiple layers of iteration nest together and only one condition demands an immediate stop, throw and catch present a direct solution. A synergy with previously learned rescue blocks can emerge if data validation fails, but that scenario typically relates to actual error states. Meanwhile, catch and throw handles the logic of immediate exits for routine flow decisions, keeping exceptions reserved for genuine error conditions.

Summary

In short, we found that errors didn't always mean total failure. Instead, they created chances to control how the app reacted. By focusing on raising exceptions, developers could clearly show when normal flow couldn't continue. This prompted rescue blocks to step in and handle unexpected situations. These methods made sure that even if a file read or calculation failed, the script could handle resources or try again. It was also discovered that custom error classes could convey domain-specific issues more precisely, enhancing organization within larger projects.

There was also an understanding that final tasks could run regardless of success or failure, thanks to the ensure block. This construct provided reassurance that open connections would close, memory would be cleaned, and logs would finalize. Additionally, retry surfaced as a way to attempt the same operation again when disruptions were transient. When network problems or file unavailability happened, it wasn't as scary because a piece of code could pause, increment a counter, and try again. Instead of treating every obstacle as a huge deal, we could make programs that were more reliable and continued past minor issues. By using these techniques, the application's responses felt smoother, avoiding sudden stops and guiding processes along more stable paths.

CHAPTER 5: OBJECT-ORIENTED PROGRAMMING BASICS

Chapter Overview

In this chapter, you'll get to grips with the fundamentals of Ruby's object-oriented programming (OOP), giving you the skills to create and manage complex applications. You'll start by defining classes, the blueprints for objects, and learning how to instantiate and use them effectively in your programs. Then, you'll dive into access control for methods, where you'll discover how to encapsulate your code by setting methods as public, private, or protected. This control makes sure that your objects only show the interfaces you want, protecting your internal logic from outside interference and creating a clean, secure codebase.

Finally, the chapter teaches about inheritance and polymorphism, two powerful OOP principles that make your code more flexible and reusable. With inheritance, you can create a hierarchy between classes, allowing child classes to get and override behaviors from their parents. Polymorphism is another biggie, since it lets you treat objects like instances of their parent class. This makes it easier to make dynamic method calls and helps you build a more adaptable and scalable architecture. When you put these topics together, you've got a rock-solid understanding of OOP in Ruby, setting you up for more advanced programming techniques.

Defining and Using Classes

Classes form the backbone of OOP in Ruby, providing a blueprint for creating objects that encapsulate both data and behavior. In Ruby, a class is defined using the **class** keyword, followed by the class name, which by convention starts with an uppercase letter. Within the class, the **initialize** method serves as a constructor, setting up initial values for an object's instance variables. Instance variables, prefixed with **@**, hold data specific to each object instance, ensuring that each object maintains its own state independently of others.

Defining a Class and Initializing Objects

To illustrate the concept, let's extend our existing sample program by introducing a **User** class. This class will encapsulate user-related data and behaviors, making our script more organized and reflective of real-world structures.

```
# user_demo.rb
class User
  # Initialize method to set up instance variables
  def initialize(name, age, status)
    @name = name
    @age = age
```

```
    @status = status
  end
  # Method to display user information
  def display_info
    puts "Name: #{@name}"
    puts "Age: #{@age}"
    puts "Status: #{@status}"
  end
end
# Creating instances of User
user1 = User.new("Alice", 30, :active)
user2 = User.new("Bob", 25, :inactive)
# Displaying user information
user1.display_info
puts "-----"
user2.display_info
```

Here, the **User** class is defined with an **initialize** method that takes three parameters: **name**, **age**, and **status**. These parameters are assigned to instance variables **@name**, **@age**, and **@status**, respectively. The **display_info** method prints out the user's information, demonstrating how instance variables store and retrieve data specific to each object.

Sample Program: Incorporating Classes

Now let us try to integrate the **User** class into our ongoing sample program, combining it with previously defined variables, constants, and methods. You can see how this integration works by looking at how the classes interact with the other elements in the script.

```
# integrated_demo.rb
MAX_TEMPERATURE = 38.0
DEFAULT_STATUS = :inactive
class User
  def initialize(name, age, status = DEFAULT_STATUS)
```

```
    @name = name
    @age = age
    @status = status
  end
  def display_info
    puts "Name: #{@name}"
    puts "Age: #{@age}"
    puts "Status: #{@status}"
  end
  def update_status(new_status)
    @status = new_status
    puts "#{@name}'s status updated to #{@status}."
  end
end
def analyze_temperature(temp)
  raise TemperatureError, "Reading too high!" if temp >
MAX_TEMPERATURE
  puts "Temperature is normal or slightly elevated: #{temp}"
end
begin
  puts "Creating user instances."
  user1 = User.new("Alice", 30)
  user2 = User.new("Bob", 25, :active)
  puts "Displaying user information:"
  user1.display_info
  puts "-----"
  user2.display_info
  puts "Updating user status:"
  user1.update_status(:active)
```

```ruby
  puts "-----"
  puts "Analyzing temperatures:"
  readings = [36.5, 37.2, 38.5, 39.1, 40.0]
  readings.each do |temp|
    analyze_temperature(temp)
  end
rescue TemperatureError => e
  puts "Caught a temperature problem: #{e.message}"
ensure
  puts "Finalizing user data."
end
puts "Program continues..."
```

Now in the above script, the **User** class interacts seamlessly with other components. The **initialize** method now includes a default value for the **status** parameter, utilizing the **DEFAULT_STATUS** constant. The **update_status** method allows modifying a user's status dynamically, demonstrating encapsulation by keeping the status management within the **User** class. The **analyze_temperature** method, previously learned in error handling, now works alongside the **User** class. When a temperature exceeds **MAX_TEMPERATURE**, a **TemperatureError** is raised, and the rescue block catches and handles it gracefully. This whole combination of classes and error handling illustrates how different Ruby features can collaborate to build robust and maintainable applications.

Access Control for Methods

In Ruby, managing how methods are accessed is crucial for maintaining a clean and secure codebase. Without proper access control, any part of a program could inadvertently modify or invoke methods that should remain internal, leading to unpredictable behaviors and potential bugs.

Consider a scenario where a class handles sensitive data processing; exposing all its methods publicly might allow external entities to manipulate internal states improperly. For instance, a **User** class might have methods that update user status or display information. While some methods should be accessible to any part of the program (public), others might only be relevant within the class itself (private) or by subclasses (protected). If developers clearly define these boundaries, they can enforce encapsulation, a key principle of OOP. This promotes modularity and reduces interdependencies within the code.

Public, Private, and Protected Methods

Ruby categorizes methods based on their accessibility:

- **Public Methods**: These methods can be called by any object. By default, all methods in Ruby are public unless specified otherwise. Public methods define the interface through which objects interact with each other.
- **Private Methods**: These methods cannot be called with an explicit receiver. They are intended for internal use within the class, ensuring that certain functionalities remain hidden from external access. Private methods are useful for encapsulating helper functions that should not be exposed as part of the class's public API.
- **Protected Methods**: These methods can be called by any instance of the defining class or its subclasses, but not by external objects. Protected methods are useful when you need to allow access to certain methods within a family of related classes without exposing them publicly.

When you understand and apply these access levels the right way, you can design solid and easy-to-maintain classes. You can also prevent unexpected interactions and protect the internal logic of your objects.

Sample Program: Implementing Access Control

We continue our same sample program and we now define public methods for interacting with user data, private methods for internal computations, and protected methods for operations that should only be accessible within the class hierarchy.

```
# integrated_demo.rb
MAX_TEMPERATURE = 38.0
DEFAULT_STATUS = :inactive
class TemperatureError < StandardError; end
class User
  attr_reader :name, :age, :status
  def initialize(name, age, status = DEFAULT_STATUS)
    @name = name
    @age = age
    @status = status
  end
```

```
  # Public method to display user information
  def display_info
    puts "Name: #{@name}"
    puts "Age: #{@age}"
    puts "Status: #{@status}"
  end
  # Public method to update user status
  def update_status(new_status)
    @status = new_status
    puts "#{@name}'s status updated to #{@status}."
  end
  # Protected method to compare user ages
  protected
  def older_than?(other_user)
    @age > other_user.age
  end
  # Private method to validate user status
  private
  def validate_status(new_status)
    valid_statuses = [:active, :inactive, :banned]
    unless valid_statuses.include?(new_status)
      raise "Invalid status: #{new_status}. Valid statuses are
#{valid_statuses.join(', ')}."
    end
  end
end
def analyze_temperature(temp)
  raise TemperatureError, "Reading too high!" if temp >
MAX_TEMPERATURE
  puts "Temperature is normal or slightly elevated: #{temp}"
```

```
end
begin
  puts "Creating user instances."
  user1 = User.new("Alice", 30)
  user2 = User.new("Bob", 25, :active)
  puts "Displaying user information:"
  user1.display_info
  puts "-----"
  user2.display_info
  puts "Updating user status:"
  user1.update_status(:active)
  puts "-----"
  puts "Comparing users:"
  if user1.older_than?(user2)
    puts "#{user1.name} is older than #{user2.name}."
  else
    puts "#{user1.name} is not older than #{user2.name}."
  end
  puts "-----"
  puts "Analyzing temperatures:"
  readings = [36.5, 37.2, 38.5, 39.1, 40.0]
  readings.each do |temp|
    analyze_temperature(temp)
  end
rescue TemperatureError => e
  puts "Caught a temperature problem: #{e.message}"
rescue => e
  puts "An error occurred: #{e.message}"
ensure
```

```
  puts "Finalizing user data."
end
puts "Program continues..."
```

Here in the above script,

- **display_info** and **update_status** are accessible from anywhere, allowing external objects or parts of the program to interact with the **User** instances. The **user1.display_info** prints user details, and **user1.update_status(:active)** changes the user's status.
- The **older_than?** method allows comparison between two **User** instances. It's marked as protected to restrict access only within the class itself or its subclasses. This method facilitates internal logic without exposing it as part of the public interface. The **user1.older_than?(user2)** compares the ages of two users, ensuring that such comparisons are controlled and meaningful within the class context.
- The **validate_status** method ensures that any status update is valid. By making it private, we prevent external code from invoking it directly, thereby safeguarding the integrity of the user's status. Although not explicitly called in the sample program, this method could be integrated into **update_status** to enforce validation rules, ensuring that only predefined statuses are assigned to users.

Improvising Program with Access Control

Now we try to refine the **User** class by integrating the **validate_status** method into **update_status**, ensuring that any status updates are validated before being applied as below.

```
class User
  attr_reader :name, :age, :status
  def initialize(name, age, status = DEFAULT_STATUS)
    @name = name
    @age = age
    @status = status
  end
  # Public method to display user information
  def display_info
    puts "Name: #{@name}"
```

```
    puts "Age: #{@age}"
    puts "Status: #{@status}"
  end
  # Public method to update user status with validation
  def update_status(new_status)
    validate_status(new_status)
    @status = new_status
    puts "#{@name}'s status updated to #{@status}."
  end
  # Protected method to compare user ages
  protected
  def older_than?(other_user)
    @age > other_user.age
  end
  # Private method to validate user status
  private
  def validate_status(new_status)
    valid_statuses = [:active, :inactive, :banned]
    unless valid_statuses.include?(new_status)
      raise "Invalid status: #{new_status}. Valid statuses are
#{valid_statuses.join(', ')}."
    end
  end
end
```

Here, invoking **validate_status** within **update_status** ensures any attempt to change a user's status adheres to predefined rules. If an invalid status is provided, the method raises an error, which can be rescued and handled appropriately in the main program flow.

Inheritance and Polymorphism

Inheritance is a huge deal in OOP. It lets classes take on the traits and behavior of other classes. In Ruby, when you make a new class, it can pick up properties and methods from an existing class (called the superclass or parent class). This makes it so you can use code over and over again, cuts down on redundancy, and organizes classes in a way that mirrors real-world relationships. For instance, if you have a general **User** class, you can create more specific classes like **AdminUser** or **GuestUser** that inherit from **User**. These subclasses can introduce additional attributes or override existing methods to cater to their unique roles while still maintaining the foundational behaviors defined in the **User** class.

Leveraging Inheritance

Let us consider a situation where we extend our existing **User** class by introducing two subclasses: **AdminUser** and **GuestUser**. These subclasses will inherit from **User** and add or modify functionalities pertinent to their specific roles.

```
# inheritance_demo.rb
class User
  attr_reader :name, :age, :status
  def initialize(name, age, status = DEFAULT_STATUS)
    @name = name
    @age = age
    @status = status
  end
  # Public method to display user information
  def display_info
    puts "Name: #{@name}"
    puts "Age: #{@age}"
    puts "Status: #{@status}"
  end
  # Public method to update user status with validation
  def update_status(new_status)
    validate_status(new_status)
    @status = new_status
    puts "#{@name}'s status updated to #{@status}."
```

```
  end
  # Protected method to compare user ages
  protected
  def older_than?(other_user)
    @age > other_user.age
  end
  # Private method to validate user status
  private
  def validate_status(new_status)
    valid_statuses = [:active, :inactive, :banned]
    unless valid_statuses.include?(new_status)
      raise "Invalid status: #{new_status}. Valid statuses are
#{valid_statuses.join(', ')}."
    end
  end
end
# Subclass for Admin Users
class AdminUser < User
  attr_reader :admin_level
  def initialize(name, age, status = DEFAULT_STATUS,
admin_level = 1)
    super(name, age, status)
    @admin_level = admin_level
  end
  # Overriding display_info to include admin_level
  def display_info
    super
    puts "Admin Level: #{@admin_level}"
  end
  # Public method specific to AdminUser
```

```
  def promote_user(user)
    if self.older_than?(user)
      user.update_status(:active)
      puts "#{user.name} has been promoted by #{self.name}."
    else
      puts "#{self.name} cannot promote #{user.name} due to
age restrictions."
    end
  end
end
# Subclass for Guest Users
class GuestUser < User
  def initialize(name, age, status = DEFAULT_STATUS)
    super(name, age, status)
  end
  # Overriding update_status to restrict status changes
  def update_status(new_status)
    puts "Guest users cannot change their status."
  end
end
```

Here in the above program, the **AdminUser** and **GuestUser** inherit from **User**. The **AdminUser** class introduces an additional attribute, **admin_level**, and overrides the **display_info** method to include this new attribute. It also adds a new method, **promote_user**, demonstrating how subclasses can introduce unique behaviors. On the other hand, **GuestUser** overrides the **update_status** method to restrict status changes, showcasing how inheritance allows subclasses to modify or restrict inherited behaviors.

Utilizing Polymorphism for Flexible Code

Polymorphism lets you treat objects of different classes related by inheritance the same way, based on their shared superclass. This means that a method can accept objects of the superclass type, but behave differently depending on the actual subclass instance it receives. Polymorphism makes things more flexible and scalable, so developers can write more generic and reusable code.

Consider a scenario where you have a method that processes different types of users. With polymorphism, this method can handle **User**, **AdminUser**, and **GuestUser** objects seamlessly, invoking the appropriate methods based on each object's class.

```
# polymorphism_demo.rb
def process_user(user)
  puts "Processing user: #{user.name}"
  user.display_info
  puts "-----"
end
# Creating instances
admin = AdminUser.new("Alice", 30, :active, 2)
guest = GuestUser.new("Bob", 25)
# Processing users
process_user(admin)
process_user(guest)
```

When **process_user** is called with an **AdminUser** instance, it invokes the overridden **display_info** method, displaying the additional **admin_level** information. Conversely, when called with a **GuestUser** instance, it invokes the **display_info** method from the **User** class without the **admin_level**. This behavior illustrates how polymorphism allows methods to interact with objects of different subclasses through a common interface, promoting code flexibility and reducing the need for type-specific conditions.

Sample Program: Integrating Inheritance and Polymorphism

Now let us try out a program where we integrate both inheritance and polymorphism into our ongoing sample program.

```
# integrated_demo.rb
MAX_TEMPERATURE = 38.0
DEFAULT_STATUS = :inactive
class TemperatureError < StandardError; end
class User
  attr_reader :name, :age, :status
```

```
  def initialize(name, age, status = DEFAULT_STATUS)
    @name = name
    @age = age
    @status = status
  end
  # Public method to display user information
  def display_info
    puts "Name: #{@name}"
    puts "Age: #{@age}"
    puts "Status: #{@status}"
  end
  # Public method to update user status with validation
  def update_status(new_status)
    validate_status(new_status)
    @status = new_status
    puts "#{@name}'s status updated to #{@status}."
  end
  # Protected method to compare user ages
  protected
  def older_than?(other_user)
    @age > other_user.age
  end
  # Private method to validate user status
  private
  def validate_status(new_status)
    valid_statuses = [:active, :inactive, :banned]
    unless valid_statuses.include?(new_status)
      raise "Invalid status: #{new_status}. Valid statuses are
#{valid_statuses.join(', ')}."
```

```
    end
  end
end
# Subclass for Admin Users
class AdminUser < User
  attr_reader :admin_level
  def initialize(name, age, status = DEFAULT_STATUS,
admin_level = 1)
    super(name, age, status)
    @admin_level = admin_level
  end
  # Overriding display_info to include admin_level
  def display_info
    super
    puts "Admin Level: #{@admin_level}"
  end
  # Public method specific to AdminUser
  def promote_user(user)
    if self.older_than?(user)
      user.update_status(:active)
      puts "#{user.name} has been promoted by #{self.name}."
    else
      puts "#{self.name} cannot promote #{user.name} due to
age restrictions."
    end
  end
end
# Subclass for Guest Users
class GuestUser < User
  def initialize(name, age, status = DEFAULT_STATUS)
```

```
    super(name, age, status)
  end
  # Overriding update_status to restrict status changes
  def update_status(new_status)
    puts "Guest users cannot change their status."
  end
end
def analyze_temperature(temp)
  raise TemperatureError, "Reading too high!" if temp >
MAX_TEMPERATURE
  puts "Temperature is normal or slightly elevated: #{temp}"
end
def process_user(user)
  puts "Processing user: #{user.name}"
  user.display_info
  puts "-----"
end
begin
  puts "Creating user instances."
  admin = AdminUser.new("Alice", 30, :active, 2)
  guest = GuestUser.new("Bob", 25)
  puts "Displaying user information:"
  process_user(admin)
  process_user(guest)
  puts "Updating user status:"
  admin.update_status(:inactive)
  guest.update_status(:active) # This will be restricted
  puts "-----"
  puts "Promoting users:"
```

```
  admin.promote_user(guest) # Attempt to promote a guest user
  puts "-----"
  puts "Analyzing temperatures:"
  readings = [36.5, 37.2, 38.5, 39.1, 40.0]
  readings.each do |temp|
    analyze_temperature(temp)
  end
rescue TemperatureError => e
  puts "Caught a temperature problem: #{e.message}"
rescue => e
  puts "An error occurred: #{e.message}"
ensure
  puts "Finalizing user data."
end
puts "Program continues..."
```

Now in the above implementation,

- The **AdminUser Subclass** extends the **User** class by adding an **admin_level** attribute. It overrides the **display_info** method to include the **admin_level**. And, it also introduces **promote_user** stating how subclasses can encapsulate behaviors pertinent to their specific roles.
- The **GuestUser Subclass** overrides the **update_status** method to restrict status changes.
- The **process_user** method accepts any object that inherits from **User**, treating **AdminUser** and **GuestUser** uniformly while allowing their unique **display_info** methods to execute appropriately.
- The **admin.promote_user(guest)** call demonstrates interaction between subclasses. Although **GuestUser** inherits from **User**, attempting to promote a guest triggers the overridden **update_status** method in **GuestUser**, which restricts the status change, showcasing how polymorphism influences method behavior across different subclasses.
- The **analyze_temperature** method, along with the **TemperatureError** exception, integrates with the class hierarchy by ensuring that temperature analysis

remains consistent across user types.

Here, when you put both of these concepts into your sample program, you showed how they're used in real life. This also highlights the advantages of a well-structured object-oriented approach.

Summary

So, to sum it up, you've got a solid grasp of OOP. You've learned to define classes and create a blueprint for objects that hold both data and behavior. By creating instances of these classes, you've explored how objects maintain their own state through instance variables, which allows you to manage data in a way that's unique to you.

Then, you've delved into access control to ensure safe and sound interactions between methods. You got to explore controlling parts of the code that can access which methods, as well as inheritance and polymorphism, which are really powerful ways to reuse code and make it flexible. So by the end of the chapter, you'll be able to become more organized and start building reusable and robust Ruby applications. All in all, this chapter gave you the tools you need to tackle more advanced programming concepts and build complex software systems.

Chapter 6: Modules and Refinements

Chapter Overview

This chapter's going to teach you all about modules and refinements in Ruby. They make a huge difference, especially when it comes to making code that's modular and easy to maintain. When you learn to include and extend modules, you'll figure out how to share reusable features across different classes without using inheritance. This approach not only follows the DRY principle (Don't Repeat Yourself), but it also makes your codebase more flexible, letting you mix in behaviors as needed.

Then, we'll dive into using **`Module#prepend`** to add or override methods in existing classes. This gives you a neater and more controlled way to enhance class behaviors, so you can change how they work without changing the original definitions. Lastly, implementing refinements gives you a scoped way to modify existing classes safely.

Including and Extending Modules

Need for Sharing Functionalities

As apps get more complex, it's key to be able to share reusable features across different classes. Keeping the same code in multiple places makes the code base bigger and makes maintenance harder. Luckily, Ruby's modules give us a great way to group together shared behaviors and mix them into different classes without using inheritance.

Now think of a scenario where both **`AdminUser`** and **`GuestUser`** need logging capabilities to track their activities. Here, instead of writing identical logging methods within each class, a module can encapsulate this functionality and be included or extended as needed. This approach reduces redundancy as well as ensures consistency in how logging is handled across different parts of the application.

Defining Modules for Reusable Functionality

We will now define a **`Logger`** module that provides logging capabilities:

```
# logger_module.rb
module Logger
  def log(message)
    puts "[LOG] #{Time.now}: #{message}"
  end
  def error_log(message)
```

```
    puts "[ERROR] #{Time.now}: #{message}"
  end
end
```

Here, two methods are defined: **log** for general logging and **error_log** for logging error messages. Both these methods can be reused across different classes, ensuring a consistent logging format and behavior.

Including Modules in Classes

When you include a module within a class, the module's methods get injected as instance methods of that class. This lets objects in the class use the shared functionalities without any hassle.

So let us now include the **Logger** module in both **User** and **AdminUser** classes:

```
# integrated_demo.rb
MAX_TEMPERATURE = 38.0
DEFAULT_STATUS = :inactive
require_relative 'logger_module'
class TemperatureError < StandardError; end
class User
  include Logger
  attr_reader :name, :age, :status
  def initialize(name, age, status = DEFAULT_STATUS)
    @name = name
    @age = age
    @status = status
    log("#{@name} has been created with status #{@status}.")
  end
  # Public method to display user information
  def display_info
    puts "Name: #{@name}"
    puts "Age: #{@age}"
    puts "Status: #{@status}"
```

```
    log("Displayed info for #{@name}.")
  end
  # Public method to update user status with validation
  def update_status(new_status)
    validate_status(new_status)
    @status = new_status
    log("#{@name}'s status updated to #{@status}.")
  end
  # Protected method to compare user ages
  protected
  def older_than?(other_user)
    @age > other_user.age
  end
  # Private method to validate user status
  private
  def validate_status(new_status)
    valid_statuses = [:active, :inactive, :banned]
    unless valid_statuses.include?(new_status)
      raise "Invalid status: #{new_status}. Valid statuses are
#{valid_statuses.join(', ')}."
    end
  end
end
# Subclass for Admin Users
class AdminUser < User
  attr_reader :admin_level
  def initialize(name, age, status = DEFAULT_STATUS,
admin_level = 1)
    super(name, age, status)
    @admin_level = admin_level
```

```
    log("#{@name} initialized with admin level
#{@admin_level}.")
  end
  # Overriding display_info to include admin_level
  def display_info
    super
    puts "Admin Level: #{@admin_level}"
    log("Displayed admin level for #{@name}.")
  end
  # Public method specific to AdminUser
  def promote_user(user)
    if self.older_than?(user)
      user.update_status(:active)
      log("#{user.name} has been promoted by #{@name}.")
    else
      log("#{@name} cannot promote #{user.name} due to age
restrictions.")
      puts "#{@name} cannot promote #{user.name} due to age
restrictions."
    end
  end
end
# Subclass for Guest Users
class GuestUser < User
  def initialize(name, age, status = DEFAULT_STATUS)
    super(name, age, status)
    log("#{@name} initialized as a Guest User.")
  end
  # Overriding update_status to restrict status changes
  def update_status(new_status)
```

```
    error_log("Attempt to change status by guest user #{@name}
is not allowed.")
    puts "Guest users cannot change their status."
  end
end
def analyze_temperature(temp)
  raise TemperatureError, "Reading too high!" if temp >
MAX_TEMPERATURE
  puts "Temperature is normal or slightly elevated: #{temp}"
end
def process_user(user)
  puts "Processing user: #{user.name}"
  user.display_info
  puts "-----"
end
begin
  puts "Creating user instances."
  admin = AdminUser.new("Alice", 30, :active, 2)
  guest = GuestUser.new("Bob", 25)
  puts "Displaying user information:"
  process_user(admin)
  process_user(guest)
  puts "Updating user status:"
  admin.update_status(:inactive)
  guest.update_status(:active) # This will be restricted
  puts "-----"
  puts "Promoting users:"
  admin.promote_user(guest) # Attempt to promote a guest user
  puts "-----"
  puts "Analyzing temperatures:"
```

```
  readings = [36.5, 37.2, 38.5, 39.1, 40.0]
  readings.each do |temp|
    analyze_temperature(temp)
  end
rescue TemperatureError => e
  puts "Caught a temperature problem: #{e.message}"
rescue => e
  puts "An error occurred: #{e.message}"
ensure
  puts "Finalizing user data."
end
puts "Program continues..."
```

Here in the above program, the **initialize** method logs the creation of a new user. Similarly, methods like **display_info** and **update_status** log relevant actions. The **AdminUser** subclass further logs its initialization and specific actions like promoting a user. The **GuestUser** class uses **error_log** to log attempts to change its status, demonstrating how different logging methods can be utilized based on the context.

Extending Modules for Class Methods

While **include** mixes in modules as instance methods, **extend** adds the module's methods as class methods. This distinction allows modules to provide both instance-level and class-level functionalities.

So let us again enhance the **Logger** module to include class methods for logging:

```
# logger_module.rb
module Logger
  def log(message)
    puts "[LOG] #{Time.now}: #{message}"
  end
  def error_log(message)
    puts "[ERROR] #{Time.now}: #{message}"
```

```
  end
  module ClassMethods
    def class_log(message)
      puts "[CLASS LOG] #{Time.now}: #{message}"
    end
  end
  def self.included(base)
    base.extend(ClassMethods)
  end
end
```

Here, in this updated **Logger** module,

- **log** and **error_log** remain as instance methods.
- The nested **ClassMethods** module contains **class_log**. And,
- The **self.included** method ensures that when **Logger** is included in a class, the class itself is extended with the **ClassMethods** module, thereby gaining access to **class_log**.

Further, we can now utilize the class-level logging within our **User** class:

```
# logger_module.rb remains the same with ClassMethods
# integrated_demo.rb
require_relative 'logger_module'
class User
  include Logger
  attr_reader :name, :age, :status
  def initialize(name, age, status = DEFAULT_STATUS)
    @name = name
    @age = age
    @status = status
    log("#{@name} has been created with status #{@status}.")
```

```
    self.class.class_log("A new user instance created:
#{@name}.")
  end
  # Public method to display user information
  def display_info
    puts "Name: #{@name}"
    puts "Age: #{@age}"
    puts "Status: #{@status}"
    log("Displayed info for #{@name}.")
  end
  # Public method to update user status with validation
  def update_status(new_status)
    validate_status(new_status)
    @status = new_status
    log("#{@name}'s status updated to #{@status}.")
  end
  # Protected method to compare user ages
  protected
  def older_than?(other_user)
    @age > other_user.age
  end
  # Private method to validate user status
  private
  def validate_status(new_status)
    valid_statuses = [:active, :inactive, :banned]
    unless valid_statuses.include?(new_status)
      raise "Invalid status: #{new_status}. Valid statuses are
#{valid_statuses.join(', ')}."
    end
  end
```

```
end
# Subclass for Admin Users
class AdminUser < User
  attr_reader :admin_level
  def initialize(name, age, status = DEFAULT_STATUS,
admin_level = 1)
    super(name, age, status)
    @admin_level = admin_level
    log("#{@name} initialized with admin level
#{@admin_level}.")
    self.class.class_log("AdminUser created: #{@name} with
admin level #{@admin_level}.")
  end
  # Overriding display_info to include admin_level
  def display_info
    super
    puts "Admin Level: #{@admin_level}"
    log("Displayed admin level for #{@name}.")
  end
  # Public method specific to AdminUser
  def promote_user(user)
    if self.older_than?(user)
      user.update_status(:active)
      log("#{user.name} has been promoted by #{@name}.")
    else
      log("#{@name} cannot promote #{user.name} due to age
restrictions.")
      puts "#{@name} cannot promote #{user.name} due to age
restrictions."
    end
  end
```

```
end
# Subclass for Guest Users
class GuestUser < User
  def initialize(name, age, status = DEFAULT_STATUS)
    super(name, age, status)
    log("#{@name} initialized as a Guest User.")
    self.class.class_log("GuestUser created: #{@name}.")
  end
  # Overriding update_status to restrict status changes
  def update_status(new_status)
    error_log("Attempt to change status by guest user #{@name}
is not allowed.")
    puts "Guest users cannot change their status."
  end
end
def analyze_temperature(temp)
  raise TemperatureError, "Reading too high!" if temp >
MAX_TEMPERATURE
  puts "Temperature is normal or slightly elevated: #{temp}"
end
def process_user(user)
  puts "Processing user: #{user.name}"
  user.display_info
  puts "-----"
end
begin
  puts "Creating user instances."
  admin = AdminUser.new("Alice", 30, :active, 2)
  guest = GuestUser.new("Bob", 25)
  puts "Displaying user information:"
```

```
  process_user(admin)
  process_user(guest)
  puts "Updating user status:"
  admin.update_status(:inactive)
  guest.update_status(:active) # This will be restricted
  puts "-----"
  puts "Promoting users:"
  admin.promote_user(guest) # Attempt to promote a guest user
  puts "-----"
  puts "Analyzing temperatures:"
  readings = [36.5, 37.2, 38.5, 39.1, 40.0]
  readings.each do |temp|
    analyze_temperature(temp)
  end
rescue TemperatureError => e
  puts "Caught a temperature problem: #{e.message}"
rescue => e
  puts "An error occurred: #{e.message}"
ensure
  puts "Finalizing user data."
end
puts "Program continues..."
```

To sum up, the **`Logger`** module in our sample program illustrates how logging can be efficiently shared across different user types, providing both instance-level and class-level logging capabilities. The ability to include and extend modules ensures that shared behaviors are centralized, making the codebase easier to manage and scale.

Using Module#prepend

'Module#prepend' Overview

Ruby offers several ways to incorporate modules into classes, with **include** and **extend** being the most common. However, **Module#prepend** provides a unique mechanism that alters the method lookup order, allowing module methods to take precedence over those in the class. This feature is particularly useful when you need to override or augment existing methods without altering the original class definitions directly. So, when a module is prepended to a class, Ruby places the module above the class in the method lookup chain. This means that methods defined in the prepended module are called before those in the class itself. Consequently, **prepend** enables more controlled and flexible modifications, especially in scenarios where multiple modules or inheritance hierarchies are involved.

Differences Between 'include' and 'prepend'

To grasp the utility of **prepend**, it's essential to understand how it contrasts with **include**:

When a module is included in a class, its methods become part of the class's method lookup chain, but they are positioned below the class itself. This setup means that if the class defines a method with the same name as one in the included module, the class's method will take precedence.

```
module Greet
  def say_hello
    puts "Hello from Greet module!"
  end
end
class Person
  include Greet
  def say_hello
    puts "Hello from Person class!"
  end
end
person = Person.new
person.say_hello
# Output: "Hello from Person class!"
```

Conversely, when a module is prepended, its methods are placed above the class in the method lookup chain. This arrangement ensures that the module's methods override those in the class.

```
module Greet
```

```
  def say_hello
    puts "Hello from Greet module!"
  end
end
class Person
  prepend Greet
  def say_hello
    puts "Hello from Person class!"
  end
end
person = Person.new
person.say_hello
# Output: "Hello from Greet module!"
```

This difference is pivotal when you need to modify or extend class behaviors without changing the class itself. **prepend** allows modules to effectively "hook into" class methods, providing a powerful tool for metaprogramming and behavior modification.

Sample Program: 'Module#prepend' Implementation

To demonstrate the practical utility of **Module#prepend**, let's extend our existing sample program by introducing a **TimestampLogger** module. This module will prepend logging functionality that adds timestamps to log messages, enhancing the existing **Logger** module's capabilities.

First, let us define the **TimestampLogger** module:

```
# timestamp_logger_module.rb
module TimestampLogger
  def log(message)
    puts "[TIMESTAMP LOG] #{Time.now}: #{message}"
  end
  def error_log(message)
    puts "[TIMESTAMP ERROR] #{Time.now}: #{message}"
```

```
  end
end
```

Next, modify the **User** class to prepend the **TimestampLogger** module instead of including the **Logger** module directly. This change ensures that the **TimestampLogger** methods take precedence over those in the **Logger** module as shown below.

```
# integrated_demo.rb
MAX_TEMPERATURE = 38.0
DEFAULT_STATUS = :inactive
require_relative 'logger_module'
require_relative 'timestamp_logger_module'
class TemperatureError < StandardError; end
class User
  prepend TimestampLogger
  include Logger
  attr_reader :name, :age, :status
  def initialize(name, age, status = DEFAULT_STATUS)
    @name = name
    @age = age
    @status = status
    log("#{@name} has been created with status #{@status}.")
    self.class.class_log("A new user instance created:
#{@name}.")
  end
  # Public method to display user information
  def display_info
    puts "Name: #{@name}"
    puts "Age: #{@age}"
    puts "Status: #{@status}"
    log("Displayed info for #{@name}.")
```

```
  end
  # Public method to update user status with validation
  def update_status(new_status)
    validate_status(new_status)
    @status = new_status
    log("#{@name}'s status updated to #{@status}.")
  end
  # Protected method to compare user ages
  protected
  def older_than?(other_user)
    @age > other_user.age
  end
  # Private method to validate user status
  private
  def validate_status(new_status)
    valid_statuses = [:active, :inactive, :banned]
    unless valid_statuses.include?(new_status)
      raise "Invalid status: #{new_status}. Valid statuses are
#{valid_statuses.join(', ')}."
    end
  end
end
# Subclass for Admin Users
class AdminUser < User
  attr_reader :admin_level
  def initialize(name, age, status = DEFAULT_STATUS,
admin_level = 1)
    super(name, age, status)
    @admin_level = admin_level
```

```
    log("#{@name} initialized with admin level
#{@admin_level}.")
    self.class.class_log("AdminUser created: #{@name} with
admin level #{@admin_level}.")
  end
  # Overriding display_info to include admin_level
  def display_info
    super
    puts "Admin Level: #{@admin_level}"
    log("Displayed admin level for #{@name}.")
  end
  # Public method specific to AdminUser
  def promote_user(user)
    if self.older_than?(user)
      user.update_status(:active)
      log("#{user.name} has been promoted by #{@name}.")
    else
      log("#{@name} cannot promote #{user.name} due to age
restrictions.")
      puts "#{@name} cannot promote #{user.name} due to age
restrictions."
    end
  end
end
# Subclass for Guest Users
class GuestUser < User
  def initialize(name, age, status = DEFAULT_STATUS)
    super(name, age, status)
    log("#{@name} initialized as a Guest User.")
    self.class.class_log("GuestUser created: #{@name}.")
```

```
  end
  # Overriding update_status to restrict status changes
  def update_status(new_status)
    error_log("Attempt to change status by guest user #{@name}
is not allowed.")
    puts "Guest users cannot change their status."
  end
end
def analyze_temperature(temp)
  raise TemperatureError, "Reading too high!" if temp >
MAX_TEMPERATURE
  puts "Temperature is normal or slightly elevated: #{temp}"
end
def process_user(user)
  puts "Processing user: #{user.name}"
  user.display_info
  puts "-----"
end
begin
  puts "Creating user instances."
  admin = AdminUser.new("Alice", 30, :active, 2)
  guest = GuestUser.new("Bob", 25)
  puts "Displaying user information:"
  process_user(admin)
  process_user(guest)
  puts "Updating user status:"
  admin.update_status(:inactive)
  guest.update_status(:active) # This will be restricted
  puts "-----"
  puts "Promoting users:"
```

```
  admin.promote_user(guest) # Attempt to promote a guest user
  puts "-----"
  puts "Analyzing temperatures:"
  readings = [36.5, 37.2, 38.5, 39.1, 40.0]
  readings.each do |temp|
    analyze_temperature(temp)
  end
rescue TemperatureError => e
  puts "Caught a temperature problem: #{e.message}"
rescue => e
  puts "An error occurred: #{e.message}"
ensure
  puts "Finalizing user data."
end
puts "Program continues..."
```

In the above program, the **TimestampLogger** module defines **log** and **error_log** methods that prepend a timestamp to log messages. In the **User** class, **TimestampLogger** is prepended using **prepend TimestampLogger**, while **Logger** is included using **include Logger**. This order places **TimestampLogger** above **Logger** in the method lookup chain, meaning the **log** and **error_log** methods from **TimestampLogger** override those from **Logger**.

Now, when **log** or **error_log** is called within the **User** class or its subclasses, Ruby first searches for these methods in the **TimestampLogger** module. If found, it uses them; otherwise, it falls back to the **Logger** module's methods.

After all this, once we run this above program, it will show that log messages now include timestamps, reflecting the **TimestampLogger** module's methods being called instead of those in **Logger**.

```
# Sample Output:
[TIMESTAMP LOG] 2025-01-03 10:00:00 +0000: Alice has been
created with status active.
[CLASS LOG] A new user instance created: Alice.
```

```
[TIMESTAMP LOG] 2025-01-03 10:00:00 +0000: Bob has been
created with status inactive.
[CLASS LOG] GuestUser created: Bob.
Processing user: Alice
Name: Alice
Age: 30
Status: active
Admin Level: 2
[TIMESTAMP LOG] 2025-01-03 10:00:00 +0000: Displayed info for
Alice.
[TIMESTAMP LOG] 2025-01-03 10:00:00 +0000: Displayed admin
level for Alice.
-----
Processing user: Bob
Name: Bob
Age: 25
Status: inactive
[TIMESTAMP LOG] 2025-01-03 10:00:00 +0000: Displayed info for
Bob.
-----
Updating user status:
[TIMESTAMP LOG] 2025-01-03 10:00:00 +0000: Alice's status
updated to inactive.
[TIMESTAMP ERROR] 2025-01-03 10:00:00 +0000: Attempt to change
status by guest user Bob is not allowed.
Guest users cannot change their status.
-----
Promoting users:
[TIMESTAMP LOG] 2025-01-03 10:00:00 +0000: Bob has been
promoted by Alice.
-----
```

```
Analyzing temperatures:
Temperature is normal or slightly elevated: 36.5
Temperature is normal or slightly elevated: 37.2
Temperature is normal or slightly elevated: 38.5
Caught a temperature problem: Reading too high!
Finalizing user data.
Program continues...
```

In the above implementation, the **TimestampLogger** module demonstrated how **prepend** can be used to override logging methods, enriching the logging output with timestamps while preserving the original **Logger** module's functionality. You should definitely use prepend along with other module-based strategies if you want to develop scalable and maintainable Ruby programs.

Implementing Refinements

Exploring Refinements

It's common for Ruby apps to grow and need to modify or extend existing classes without messing with their global behavior. But traditional methods like monkey patching can lead to unexpected side effects, making maintenance tough and possibly introducing bugs. Ruby's refinements offer a safer alternative by allowing scoped modifications to classes. Refinements let developers alter class behavior within specific contexts, making sure changes don't leak into the global scope. This makes your code cleaner and safer. Refinements work by opening a class in a module and only making changes where the module is turned on. This keeps everything contained, so you can extend or tweak features without messing up the whole application.

For example, let us consider the ongoing sample program involving **User**, **AdminUser**, and **GuestUser** classes. Suppose there's a requirement to format user names differently in certain parts of the application. While displaying user information, names should appear in uppercase, but in other contexts, the original casing should be preserved. Instead of globally modifying the **User** class to always display names in uppercase, refinements can be used to apply this formatting selectively.

Defining a Refinement Module

To implement refinements, first, define a module that contains the desired modifications. Within this module, reopen the target class and redefine or add methods as needed.

```
# name_formatter_refinement.rb
module NameFormatterRefinement
  refine User do
    def display_info
      puts "Name: #{name.upcase}"
      puts "Age: #{age}"
      puts "Status: #{status}"
      log("Displayed info for #{name.upcase}.")
    end
  end
end
```

Here in this **NameFormatterRefinement** module, the **User** class's **display_info** method is redefined to display the user's name in uppercase. By refining the **User** class within this module, the modification is scoped and does not affect the **User** class globally.

Activating Refinements

Refinements must be explicitly activated where they are intended to be used. This activation is done using the **using** keyword, which applies the refinement within the current scope.

```
# integrated_demo.rb
MAX_TEMPERATURE = 38.0
DEFAULT_STATUS = :inactive
require_relative 'logger_module'
require_relative 'timestamp_logger_module'
require_relative 'name_formatter_refinement'
class TemperatureError < StandardError; end
class User
  prepend TimestampLogger
  include Logger
  attr_reader :name, :age, :status
  def initialize(name, age, status = DEFAULT_STATUS)
```

```
    @name = name
    @age = age
    @status = status
    log("#{name} has been created with status #{status}.")
    self.class.class_log("A new user instance created:
#{name}.")
  end
  # Public method to display user information
  def display_info
    puts "Name: #{name}"
    puts "Age: #{age}"
    puts "Status: #{status}"
    log("Displayed info for #{name}.")
  end
  # Public method to update user status with validation
  def update_status(new_status)
    validate_status(new_status)
    @status = new_status
    log("#{name}'s status updated to #{status}.")
  end
  # Protected method to compare user ages
  protected
  def older_than?(other_user)
    age > other_user.age
  end
  # Private method to validate user status
  private
  def validate_status(new_status)
    valid_statuses = [:active, :inactive, :banned]
```

```
    unless valid_statuses.include?(new_status)
      raise "Invalid status: #{new_status}. Valid statuses are
#{valid_statuses.join(', ')}."
    end
  end
end
# Subclass for Admin Users
class AdminUser < User
  attr_reader :admin_level
  def initialize(name, age, status = DEFAULT_STATUS,
admin_level = 1)
    super(name, age, status)
    @admin_level = admin_level
    log("#{name} initialized with admin level
#{admin_level}.")
    self.class.class_log("AdminUser created: #{name} with
admin level #{admin_level}.")
  end
  # Overriding display_info to include admin_level
  def display_info
    super
    puts "Admin Level: #{admin_level}"
    log("Displayed admin level for #{name}.")
  end
  # Public method specific to AdminUser
  def promote_user(user)
    if older_than?(user)
      user.update_status(:active)
      log("#{user.name} has been promoted by #{name}.")
    else
```

```
      log("#{name} cannot promote #{user.name} due to age
restrictions.")
      puts "#{name} cannot promote #{user.name} due to age
restrictions."
    end
  end
end
# Subclass for Guest Users
class GuestUser < User
  def initialize(name, age, status = DEFAULT_STATUS)
    super(name, age, status)
    log("#{name} initialized as a Guest User.")
    self.class.class_log("GuestUser created: #{name}.")
  end
  # Overriding update_status to restrict status changes
  def update_status(new_status)
    error_log("Attempt to change status by guest user #{name}
is not allowed.")
    puts "Guest users cannot change their status."
  end
end
def analyze_temperature(temp)
  raise TemperatureError, "Reading too high!" if temp >
MAX_TEMPERATURE
  puts "Temperature is normal or slightly elevated: #{temp}"
end
def process_user(user)
  puts "Processing user: #{user.name}"
  user.display_info
  puts "-----"
```

```
end
begin
  puts "Creating user instances."
  admin = AdminUser.new("Alice", 30, :active, 2)
  guest = GuestUser.new("Bob", 25)
  puts "Displaying user information without refinement:"
  process_user(admin)
  process_user(guest)
  puts "-----"
  puts "Displaying user information with refinement:"
  using NameFormatterRefinement
  process_user(admin)
  process_user(guest)
  puts "-----"
  puts "Updating user status:"
  admin.update_status(:inactive)
  guest.update_status(:active) # This will be restricted
  puts "-----"
  puts "Promoting users:"
  admin.promote_user(guest) # Attempt to promote a guest user
  puts "-----"
  puts "Analyzing temperatures:"
  readings = [36.5, 37.2, 38.5, 39.1, 40.0]
  readings.each do |temp|
    analyze_temperature(temp)
  end
rescue TemperatureError => e
  puts "Caught a temperature problem: #{e.message}"
rescue => e
```

```
  puts "An error occurred: #{e.message}"
ensure
  puts "Finalizing user data."
end
puts "Program continues..."
```

In the above implementation,

- The **NameFormatterRefinement** module refines the **User** class by overriding the **display_info** method to display the user's name in uppercase.
- The **using NameFormatterRefinement** statement activates the refinement within the current scope. After this activation, any calls to **display_info** on **User** instances within this scope will use the refined version, displaying names in uppercase.
- When **process_user(admin)** and **process_user(guest)** are called without the refinement, the original **display_info** method is used, displaying names with their original casing. After activating the refinement with **using NameFormatterRefinement**, subsequent calls to **process_user** utilize the refined **display_info** method, showing names in uppercase.

This whole approach of refinements maintains the original class behavior globally. By leveraging modules and refinements together, Ruby applications can achieve greater flexibility, maintainability, and clarity.

Summary

So, you took a look at Ruby's modules and improvements to make code more modular and easy to maintain. You saw how modules can group together reusable features like logging so you can share them across different classes without repeating yourself. You also learned how to include and extend modules to inject both instance and class methods into classes, which helps follow the DRY principle and makes the code base more clean and organized.

The chapter taught Module#prepend, which changes the order that methods are looked up so that module methods are prioritized over class methods. This lets you override methods in a controlled way, which is a flexible way to change how a class works without changing the class definition. By looking at some practical examples, you saw how prepending modules can improve functionalities, like adding timestamps to log messages, so that these improvements take priority during method calls.

It also showed how refinements could be used to make changes to existing classes safely. By defining refinements, developers could apply changes in specific contexts, preventing global side effects and maintaining the integrity of the original class behavior. Overall, this chapter gave developers some pretty advanced techniques for sharing and modifying functionalities in Ruby, making their apps more flexible and robust.

CHAPTER 7: ADVANCED METHODS AND METAPROGRAMMING

Chapter Overview

In this chapter, we learn to write more dynamic and flexible code by exploring methods like **eval** and **define_method** that can teach you to execute code from strings and dynamically define methods at runtime. Next, we will learn to access and manipulate an object's state dynamically. Understanding how to interact with objects at a meta-level opens up possibilities for introspection and modification, allowing you to create more intelligent and responsive applications. This includes techniques for probing an object's attributes and methods, as well as altering them on the fly to suit specific needs.

Finally, the chapter teaches about building DSLs using metaprogramming. With some practical examples, you'll learn how to design and implement DSLs that make complex tasks easier and improve how readable your Ruby programs are. When you try these advanced methods and metaprogramming techniques, you'll gain the skills to write more dynamic, efficient, and maintainable Ruby code, which will help you get the most out of your applications.

Using 'eval' and 'define_method'

Ruby's flexibility shines through when code can adapt to new scenarios at runtime. There are two techniques such as **eval** and **define_method** that offer the power to interpret strings as code, build methods on the fly, or alter existing classes based on real-time inputs. This capability proves valuable for advanced scripting tasks, where generating or modifying logic at runtime simplifies workflows that would otherwise require repetitive boilerplate.

Exploring 'eval'

An **eval** accepts a string and evaluates it as Ruby code within the current binding. This creates dynamic statements, runs user-defined scripts, or assemble logic when static definitions are insufficient. A developer might craft specialized commands based on user inputs or configuration files. An example might appear if the system wants to enable or disable particular features by name, although ensuring that external strings are sanitized remains essential. The code snippet below showcases a basic usage of **eval** to dynamically update or call existing logic in our sample program, demonstrating how **eval** can parse a string to define or modify behavior.

Using 'define_method'

The **define_method** belongs to Ruby's metaprogramming arsenal, creating methods dynamically within a class or module. Instead of writing out each method by hand, you can loop through a list of attributes or operations, generating methods automatically. This pattern helps reduce repetition and fosters DRY principles. When combined with existing classes like **User**, **AdminUser**, or **GuestUser**, it simplifies adding specialized behaviors or responding to events without cluttering the code. A scenario might involve selectively enabling methods in

AdminUser based on admin level or allowing **User** objects to hold additional attributes on demand.

Sample Program: Integrating 'eval'

Below, our ongoing sample program is extended to show how **eval** might be used safely and purposefully:

```
# dynamic_demo.rb
require_relative 'logger_module'
require_relative 'timestamp_logger_module'
require_relative 'name_formatter_refinement'
MAX_TEMPERATURE = 38.0
DEFAULT_STATUS = :inactive
class TemperatureError < StandardError; end
# Original classes from the ongoing sample
class User
  prepend TimestampLogger
  include Logger
  attr_reader :name, :age, :status
  def initialize(name, age, status = DEFAULT_STATUS)
    @name = name
    @age = age
    @status = status
    log("#{name} has been created with status #{status}.")
    self.class.class_log("A new user instance created:
#{name}.")
  end
  def display_info
    puts "Name: #{name}"
    puts "Age: #{age}"
    puts "Status: #{status}"
```

```
    log("Displayed info for #{name}.")
  end
  def update_status(new_status)
    validate_status(new_status)
    @status = new_status
    log("#{name}'s status updated to #{status}.")
  end
  protected
  def older_than?(other_user)
    age > other_user.age
  end
  private
  def validate_status(new_status)
    valid_statuses = [:active, :inactive, :banned]
    unless valid_statuses.include?(new_status)
      raise "Invalid status: #{new_status}. Valid statuses are
#{valid_statuses.join(', ')}."
    end
  end
end
class AdminUser < User
  attr_reader :admin_level
  def initialize(name, age, status = DEFAULT_STATUS,
admin_level = 1)
    super(name, age, status)
    @admin_level = admin_level
    log("#{name} initialized with admin level
#{admin_level}.")
    self.class.class_log("AdminUser created: #{name} with
admin level #{admin_level}.")
```

```
  end
  def display_info
    super
    puts "Admin Level: #{admin_level}"
    log("Displayed admin level for #{name}.")
  end
  def promote_user(user)
    if older_than?(user)
      user.update_status(:active)
      log("#{user.name} has been promoted by #{name}.")
    else
      log("#{name} cannot promote #{user.name} due to age
restrictions.")
      puts "#{name} cannot promote #{user.name} due to age
restrictions."
    end
  end
end
class GuestUser < User
  def initialize(name, age, status = DEFAULT_STATUS)
    super(name, age, status)
    log("#{name} initialized as a Guest User.")
    self.class.class_log("GuestUser created: #{name}.")
  end
  def update_status(new_status)
    error_log("Attempt to change status by guest user #{name}
is not allowed.")
    puts "Guest users cannot change their status."
  end
end
```

```
def analyze_temperature(temp)
  raise TemperatureError, "Reading too high!" if temp >
MAX_TEMPERATURE
  puts "Temperature is normal or slightly elevated: #{temp}"
end
# A demonstration of 'eval' usage
def dynamic_evaluation(user, script)
  log_message = "[DYNAMIC EVAL] Evaluating script for
#{user.name}"
  puts log_message
  user.log(log_message)
  eval(script)
end
def process_user(user)
  puts "Processing user: #{user.name}"
  user.display_info
  puts "-----"
end
begin
  admin = AdminUser.new("Alice", 35, :active, 2)
  guest = GuestUser.new("Bob", 25)
  # Evaluate a string that updates the user's age
  # The string references 'admin' directly, which is in scope
here
  script_content = <<~SCRIPT
    admin.instance_variable_set("@age", 40)
    puts "Admin's age updated to: \#{admin.age}"
  SCRIPT
  dynamic_evaluation(admin, script_content)
  puts "Displaying user after dynamic update:"
```

```
  process_user(admin)
  # Attempt to change status for a GuestUser via eval
  script_for_guest = "guest.update_status(:active)"
  dynamic_evaluation(guest, script_for_guest)
rescue TemperatureError => e
  puts "Caught a temperature problem: #{e.message}"
rescue => e
  puts "An error occurred: #{e.message}"
ensure
  puts "Wrap-up actions."
end
```

Now here,

- **eval(script_content)** runs the string as Ruby code, changing the **@age** of **admin**.
- Variables like **admin** are accessible inside **eval** because they exist in the current scope.
- And the potential for harm is mitigated by controlling content of **script_content**.

Sample Program: Demonstrating 'define_method'

In the below sample program, we extend the code with **define_method** to showcase dynamic creation of methods for users. Suppose we want to add a suite of convenience methods that retrieve certain instance variables in a read-only fashion. Instead of manually writing them out, we can define them at runtime:

```
# define_method_demo.rb
class User
  # Existing code remains unchanged
  # Dynamically define read-only accessors for a list of
attributes
  [:name, :age, :status].each do |attr|
    define_method("read_#{attr}") do
      instance_variable_get("@#{attr}")
```

```
    end
  end
  # Additional dynamic method to check if user is a certain
status
  define_method("status?") do |desired_status|
    @status == desired_status
  end
end
# Testing define_method usage
begin
  admin = AdminUser.new("Carol", 40, :active, 3)
  puts "Admin read_name: #{admin.read_name}"
  puts "Admin read_age: #{admin.read_age}"
  puts "Admin read_status: #{admin.read_status}"
  puts "Is Admin active?: #{admin.status?(:active)}"
rescue => e
  puts "An error occurred: #{e.message}"
end
```

Here in the above script,

- The **define_method** uses a symbol or string to designate the method name and a block to define its implementation.
- The **instance_variable_get("@#{attr}")** fetches the value of an instance variable.

While **eval** and **define_method** grant impressive power, mindful usage is something we have a keep tab on it to avoid the security risk and the challenges of maintainability.

Accessing Object State Dynamically

Introspection Overview

One cool thing about Ruby is that it's dynamic, which means you can look inside objects and interact with their internals at runtime. We call this "introspection," and it lets developers check attributes, find methods, and even change values without needing a set interface to start with. Sometimes, introspection can cut down on the amount of repetitive getter/setter methods you need, or it might help you debug by showing you hidden states. But, you know, be careful—if you are not using it right, it might mess up your design.

One powerful tool for introspection is **instance_variable_get**, a method that retrieves the value of an instance variable by name. Instead of calling a dedicated getter method, developers can supply the instance variable's symbol (like **:@name**) to obtain its current contents. This approach provides a direct route to object attributes, bypassing class-level access controls. Although convenient, it circumvents traditional encapsulation, so design decisions should weigh whether this is necessary for the task at hand. For example, **instance_variable_get("@age")** might help when building debugging utilities or script-based manipulations, but it can also expose fields that were intended to remain private.

Sample Program: Implementing 'instance_variable_get'

The following is a sample that extends our existing codebase to show how **instance_variable_get** might be used for reporting or debugging. For example, let's say we want a helper method that prints out an object's internal state without relying on accessor methods:

```
# introspection_demo.rb
require_relative 'dynamic_demo'  # Our existing program with
User, AdminUser, GuestUser
def introspect_object(obj)
  puts "Introspecting object of type: #{obj.class}"
  vars = obj.instance_variables
  vars.each do |var|
    value = obj.instance_variable_get(var)
    puts "#{var}: #{value}"
  end
  puts "-----"
end
begin
  admin = AdminUser.new("Eva", 28, :active, 3)
  guest = GuestUser.new("Tony", 22)
```

```
  puts "Performing object introspection on AdminUser:"
  introspect_object(admin)
  puts "Performing object introspection on GuestUser:"
  introspect_object(guest)
rescue => e
  puts "An error occurred: #{e.message}"
end
```

Here in the above sample program,

- The **introspect_object** method loops through each instance variable in an object using **obj.instance_variables**, which returns an array of symbols representing variables (e.g., **:@name**, **:@age**).
- **obj.instance_variable_get(var)** fetches the value for each variable, printing them for inspection.

In a production environment, one might prefer a more formal debugging or logging pattern. However, this above script demonstrates how **instance_variable_get** allows you to quickly capture or manipulate data. Since **instance_variable_get** is a powerful tool, it's wise to limit it to debugging, specialized scripting, or advanced metaprogramming contexts.

I am providing you a short script that illustrates how introspection might blend into an error-handling block as below:

```
begin
  user = AdminUser.new("Nina", 45, :active, 5)
  # Simulating a scenario where no error is raised.
  puts "Simulating normal operations with user: #{user.name}"
rescue => e
  # If an error occurred, introspect the user object for
debugging
  puts "Error encountered: #{e.message}"
  puts "Inspecting user state for debugging..."
  introspect_object(user) unless user.nil?
end
```

Here, when an exception occurs, the snippet calls **introspect_object(user)** to capture the user's internal variables. This can further help to gather immediate state data at the time of failure, simplifying subsequent debugging or logging.

Building DSLs with Metaprogramming

Domain-Specific Languages (DSLs) Overview

So, when it comes to understanding DSLs in Ruby, it's usually a good idea to start by thinking about creating a mini-language that's focused on a specific problem area. If you narrow down the commands and syntax, the code becomes easier to read, and you can map it directly to business rules or specialized processes.With a DSL, you can turn repetitive tasks or configuration details into a simpler format that's almost like a human-readable version. This makes it easier for others to understand, even if they're not part of the main codebase. Now in Ruby, features like dynamic method creation, reflection, and refinements encourage developers to shape DSLs without losing the elegance of the host language.Another key point is clarity. A DSL should not only solve a problem, it should also be easy for people to understand and maintain. So, the key to creating a DSL is striking a balance between expressive constructs and minimal overhead. This results in a tool that aligns with the goals of a given domain.

Designing a Basic DSL

For example, if the main focus is on configuring user permissions, one might imagine something like:

```
configure_user "Alice" do
  role :admin
  can :promote_users
  can :manage_settings
end
```

This above script reads almost like a standard script in plain text, but behind the scenes, Ruby interprets these calls to create or modify objects. A method could define a **UserConfiguration** object, store the user's name, and collect privileges or roles. Metaprogramming techniques let the DSL capture these calls, transform them into method invocations, and configure real objects. Ruby's flexible syntax lets you omit parentheses, making the code look more like a domain-specific script. You can use blocks really powerfully, since the code inside them can run in a specially designed context (like a proxy object or an instance_eval environment) that shapes how calls are interpreted. This style makes for a flexible structure but just be careful not to go overboard and make things too confusing for other developers.

Sample Program: Implementing a DSL

You can weave an illustration of DSL building into the existing user management scenario. Let's say you want to define user objects, roles, or privileges through a specialized syntax. If you mix metaprogramming into the script, the code can parse calls that appear domain-specific, ultimately creating **User**, **AdminUser**, or **GuestUser** objects with minimal fuss:

```
# user_dsl.rb
require_relative 'dynamic_demo'  # Contains our User,
AdminUser, and GuestUser classes
module UserDSL
  def user(name, &block)
    config = UserConfiguration.new(name)
    config.instance_eval(&block) if block
    create_user_from_config(config)
  end
  class UserConfiguration
    attr_reader :name, :role, :age, :status, :admin_level
    def initialize(name)
      @name = name
      @role = :guest
      @age = 30
      @status = :inactive
      @admin_level = 1
    end
    # DSL methods
    def as_role(role_symbol)
      @role = role_symbol
    end
    def with_age(user_age)
      @age = user_age
    end
```

```
    def with_status(new_status)
      @status = new_status
    end
    def admin_level(level)
      @admin_level = level
    end
  end
  def create_user_from_config(config)
    case config.role
    when :admin
      AdminUser.new(config.name, config.age, config.status,
config.admin_level)
    when :guest
      GuestUser.new(config.name, config.age, config.status)
    else
      User.new(config.name, config.age, config.status)
    end
  end
end
# A demonstration of how this DSL might be used
class DSLExample
  extend UserDSL
  def self.build_users
    user("Alice") do
      as_role :admin
      with_age 35
      with_status :active
      admin_level 2
    end
```

```ruby
    user("Bob") do
      as_role :guest
      with_age 25
    end
    user("Carol") do
      with_age 45
      with_status :banned
    end
  end
end
puts "Constructing users with the DSL..."
created_users = DSLExample.build_users
puts "Users constructed: #{created_users.inspect}"
```

In this file, **UserDSL** defines two key concepts:

- A **UserConfiguration** class to store user attributes as they are defined in the DSL.
- A **user** method that yields a block to **UserConfiguration** and, upon completion, decides which user type to instantiate.

By calling, the code sets up a user named Alice, capturing custom details about role, age, and status as shown below:

```ruby
user("Alice") do
  as_role :admin
  with_age 35
  with_status :active
  admin_level 2
end
```

The end result is an **AdminUser** instance constructed according to the DSL instructions. Notice how the block-based syntax remains readable. The advantage is that the domain logic—defining attributes relevant to a user—flows like a mini-language while still resting on standard Ruby.

Summary

So, you figured out how to use Ruby's metaprogramming features to create flexible code that can adapt to changing requirements. You also learned how "eval" can interpret strings as runnable code, letting you modify objects on the fly or process user inputs dynamically. You checked out "define_method," which lets you construct methods in a loop or based on different conditions, cutting down on repetitive blocks of code. That technique made things a lot more flexible, since you could generate multiple specialized methods without having to write each one manually.

You then checked out "instance_variable_get," a tool for accessing an object's private data, which could help with debugging, bulk inspection, or special scripting tasks. You wrapped things up by exploring how these methods came together to create DSLs that looked like concise instructions instead of standard Ruby code. This metaprogramming-based method balanced freedom and maintainability. It created scripts that could handle unique situations, while still aligning with Ruby's philosophy of elegance. You can apply these methods to streamline your code and adapt functionality to real-world demands.

CHAPTER 8: BUILT-IN CLASSES AND MODULES

Chapter Overview

Ruby has a bunch of built-in classes and modules that form the basis of the language, affecting everything from object creation to method lookups. In this chapter, you'll check out how Object, Module, and Kernel are at the heart of Ruby's model, setting essential standards that all classes inherit. You'll learn about how methods are available across different scopes, why classes can be nested under modules, and how Kernel provides methods that feel like language features. You'll learn how each of these components works together to make up Ruby's flexible object system. This system allows for patterns ranging from simple inheritance to more advanced metaprogramming techniques.

Then, you'll check out how Enumerable and Comparable make iteration and comparison simpler across collections and custom classes. If your objects meet the method requirements, they'll be able to use features like sort, map, min, max, and more. This approach keeps your code clean and readable. And finally, you'll check out how Ruby handles regular expressions, pattern matching, text processing, and all sorts of string manipulations. When you put these topics together, you'll see just how solid the underpinnings of the language are. This'll empower you to tap into ready-made capabilities without having to reinvent the wheel.

Object, Module, and Kernel

Ruby's class hierarchy traces back to a few fundamental pillars that govern all objects in the language. At the top sits the **`Object`** class, from which nearly everything inherits. This structure provides basic methods such as **`to_s`** or **`object_id`**, and it defines how instances store their state. In practical terms, every object shares a relationship through this common ancestor, letting you call universal methods whether you are dealing with a string, a numeric type, or a user-defined class. The result is a cohesive system where polymorphism thrives, and minimal code can yield broad impacts across the entire hierarchy.

Alongside **`Object`**, you will find **`Module`**, a construct that groups methods and constants. Classes themselves are modules with added features for instantiation. By harnessing the flexibility of **`Module`**, you can mix in shared functionalities without forcing rigid inheritance structures. Another key piece, **`Kernel`**, acts like a mixin, delivering methods commonly associated with the language, such as **`puts`**, **`print`**, and **`gets`**. Although you might treat these as built-in functions, they actually come from **`Kernel`**, blended into **`Object`** so every Ruby object can access them. This arrangement showcases the language's knack for merging convenience with a modular design.

Exploring 'Object' Class

The **`Object`** class sits at the root of Ruby's inheritance tree, meaning all classes eventually derive from it. A few methods you will come across are:

- **to_s**: This converts an object to a string representation, and you can override this to refine how your custom objects appear.
- **object_id**: This one gives you an identifier for a particular object in memory.
- **methods**: This returns an array of method names available to an object, including inherited ones.

Let us take an example to explore the Object class better:

```
class CustomEntity
  def initialize(name)
    @name = name
  end
  def to_s
    "Entity Name: #{@name}"
  end
end
entity = CustomEntity.new("Demo")
puts entity.to_s                    # => "Entity Name: Demo"
puts entity.object_id               # => Some integer ID
puts entity.methods.include?(:to_s)  # => true
```

Here, your class automatically gains a wide set of methods. Overriding **to_s** adjusts how your objects appear in logs or string contexts, letting you tailor them to your domain without rebuilding from scratch.

Kernel's Omnipresent Methods

Kernel stands out because it feels like a built-in suite of commands, but it is in fact a module mixed into **Object**. Methods like **puts**, **p**, and **print** come from **Kernel**, meaning all objects can use them without explicit imports. You can call **Kernel.puts** directly, or you can rely on the fact that **Kernel** is included in the ancestry chain:

```
module Kernel
  def custom_alert(msg)
    puts "[ALERT] #{msg.upcase}"
  end
```

```
end
custom_alert("System check initiated")
```

Here, the **custom_alert** becomes available everywhere in your Ruby code once it's defined. This pattern is powerful yet demands caution, because modifying **Kernel** can affect the entire environment. Typically, adding new global methods is only advisable for domain-wide features or debugging utilities that must be accessible in any scope. Overall, you got the chance to see how Ruby's core classes and modules furnish a powerful base for any code you write.

Enumerable and Comparable Modules

Enumerable Module

Ruby's standard library provides two modules—**Enumerable** and **Comparable**—that simplify how you process collections and compare objects. By including **Enumerable**, a class gains powerful iteration methods such as **each**, **map**, **select**, and **reduce**, among many others, provided that you define **each** method for that class. A typical scenario involves arrays or hashes, but you can also include **Enumerable** in custom classes that act like collections, thereby extending them with a broad suite of functionality. This pattern underscores Ruby's preference for composable and expressive code.

Meanwhile, **Comparable** focuses on comparing objects by providing operators such as **<**, **<=**, **==**, **>=**, and **>**, along with the **between?** method. You only need to define the **<=>** operator (the "spaceship" method) in your class, and **Comparable** handles the rest. This arrangement ensures consistent comparison logic for custom objects. For instance, you might write a method that compares user ages or priorities.

Sample Program: Enumerable in Practice

Let us consider a scenario with an array of numeric data. By virtue of being an **Array**, it includes **Enumerable**, granting access to methods like **map**, **select**, **each_with_index**, and others:

```
numbers = [1, 2, 3, 4, 5]
# Using 'map' to transform each element
squares = numbers.map { |n| n * n }
puts "Squares: #{squares.inspect}"  # => [1, 4, 9, 16, 25]
# Using 'select' to filter out only even numbers
```

```ruby
evens = numbers.select { |n| n.even? }
puts "Even numbers: #{evens.inspect}"  # => [2, 4]
# Using 'reduce' to compute the sum of all elements
sum = numbers.reduce(0) { |acc, n| acc + n }
puts "Sum of numbers: #{sum}"  # => 15
```

Methods like **all?**, **none?**, **find**, **sort**, and **group_by** further expand your expressive range. For instance, **numbers.all? { |n| n > 0 }** quickly checks if all elements are positive. The key concept is that enumerators let you focus on what you want to accomplish (filtering, mapping, or aggregating) instead of writing manual loops. If you craft a custom class that acts like a collection (for example, a user-defined data container), you can include **Enumerable** and define **each** to yield elements, instantly unlocking these methods.

Comparable for Custom Comparisons

Now here, to see how **Comparable** works, imagine a class that represents temperature readings. By defining **<=>**, you can compare readings using standard operators:

```ruby
class TemperatureReading
  include Comparable
  attr_reader :value
  def initialize(value)
    @value = value
  end
  # Spaceship operator for comparison
  def <=>(other)
    @value <=> other.value
  end
end
t1 = TemperatureReading.new(37.2)
t2 = TemperatureReading.new(38.5)
puts t1 < t2    # => true
puts t1 == t2   # => false
```

```
puts t2 > t1    # => true
```

Here, **t1 < t2** translates to **t1.value < t2.value**, thanks to **Comparable**. You can also call **t1.between?(TemperatureReading.new(36), TemperatureReading.new(38))** to check if **t1** falls within a certain range.

Combination of Enumerable and Comparable

Taking further our existing sample program, we can integrate both the modules. So, let us say that you have a collection of **User** objects that you'd like to iterate over, filter, or sort by age or name:

```
class UserCollection
  include Enumerable
  def initialize(users = [])
    @users = users
  end
  # Provide the 'each' method so Enumerable can do its job
  def each
    @users.each { |u| yield u }
  end
  # Return the current list of users
  def to_a
    @users
  end
end
class User
  include Comparable
  attr_reader :name, :age
  def initialize(name, age)
    @name = name
    @age = age
  end
  def <=>(other)
```

```
    @age <=> other.age
  end
end
# Example usage
users = UserCollection.new([
  User.new("Alice", 30),
  User.new("Bob", 25),
  User.new("Carol", 35),
])
older_than_25 = users.select { |u| u.age > 25 }
puts "Users older than 25:
#{older_than_25.map(&:name).inspect}"  # => ["Alice", "Carol"]
sorted_users = users.sort  # Sort by age, since that's how
'<=>' is defined
puts "Sorted by age: #{sorted_users.map(&:name).inspect}"  #
=> ["Bob", "Alice", "Carol"]
```

In the above scenario, **UserCollection** includes **Enumerable**, letting you call methods like **select**, **map**, and **sort** on it. Meanwhile, **User** includes **Comparable**, relying on **<=>** to compare ages. Sorting then becomes a straightforward call, no manual sorting logic required.

Sample Program: Leveraging Enumerable and Comparable

Let us say you are working on the main script of the program, you might want an array or a specialized container for **AdminUser** and **GuestUser** objects. If you define **each**, you can chain enumerator methods for reporting or filtering. If you define **<=>**, you can quickly locate the oldest user or rank them by status. So, suppose you want to produce a summary that identifies which users have a certain status:

```
all_users = [AdminUser.new("Alice", 35, :active, 2),
GuestUser.new("Bob", 25, :inactive)]
active_users = all_users.select { |u| u.status == :active }
puts "Active Users: #{active_users.map(&:name).inspect}"
```

You can also include **Comparable** in **AdminUser** or **GuestUser** if you decide that these classes need a consistent way to compare instances by age, role, or another attribute. By including

Enumerable and **Comparable** in your classes, these modules minimize repetitive logic and keep your codebase consistent.

Using Regular Expressions

Introduction to Regular Expressions

An appreciation for pattern matching often leads to the exploration of regular expressions (regex), a feature that scans text for sequences of characters matching specific criteria. A short piece of syntax such as **/\w+@\w+\.\w+/** might represent a basic pattern for detecting email-like strings. An individual might use regex to validate user input, parse log files, or cleanse data for further processing. The key lies in understanding tokens like **\d** for digits, **\w** for word characters, or **.** for any character. An optional **+** or ***** can repeat parts of the expression, while anchors like **^** or **$** mark the start or end of a line. These building blocks, when combined, empower you to address text-related challenges concisely.

Using Regex for Pattern Matching and Text Manipulation

Let's say we need to check if a string matches a certain pattern, like making sure an email format is right. Given below is a sample program to get you started:

```
pattern = /\A\w+@\w+\.\w+\z/
email = "demo@example.com"
if email.match?(pattern)
  puts "Valid email format"
else
  puts "Invalid email format"
end
```

In the above, this highlights how **match?** returns a boolean indicating whether the text meets the criteria of the regular expression. Alternatively, you can use **=~** for a simpler check:

```
puts "Matches!" if email =~ pattern
```

A more in-depth use case might involve capturing groups and performing substitutions. For example, **sub** or **gsub** can replace or transform text based on patterns:

```
sanitized = "Hello, World!".gsub(/[^\w\s]/, "")
```

```
puts sanitized  # => "Hello World"
```

In the above example, punctuation is stripped out, leaving only letters, numbers, and whitespace. If you need more sophisticated parsing, capturing groups with parentheses can isolate segments of text for further handling. If we reference **`Regexp.last_match`** or use the named captures like **`/(?<user>\w+)@(?<host>\w+\.\w+)/`**, you can dissect strings methodically.

Sample Program: Integrating Regex

Let us consider that our program's **`User`** objects require validation of a nickname or handle. Instead of writing multiple string checks, a regex can confirm that the handle contains only letters, digits, or underscores as shown below:

```
class User
  VALID_HANDLE_PATTERN = /\A[a-zA-Z0-9_]+\z/
  def initialize(name, age, status = :inactive, handle = nil)
    @name = name
    @age = age
    @status = status
    if handle && handle.match?(VALID_HANDLE_PATTERN)
      @handle = handle
    else
      @handle = "guest_#{rand(1000..9999)}"
    end
    # ...rest of the code
  end
end
```

In the above script, the constructor verifies that the proposed handle matches the pattern **`\A[a-zA-Z0-9_]+\z`**. If it doesn't, a fallback generates a simple handle. Similar ideas could validate format, ensure names do not contain prohibited characters, or prevent injection attacks in a multi-user environment.

Regex also proves invaluable when searching logs or messages for keywords. So suppose **`AdminUser`** tracks suspicious activities; a method like the below one filters lines based on the provided pattern, enabling quick isolation of relevant entries.:

```
def scan_activity_logs(logs, pattern)
  logs.each_with_index do |log, idx|
    if log =~ pattern
      puts "Alert: Found match in log #{idx}: #{log}"
    end
  end
end
```

Here, each approach demonstrates that whether you are verifying text, sanitizing input, or searching for keywords, regular expressions shorten code while increasing clarity.

Summary

To sum it up, we saw how Object, Module, and Kernel worked together to determine how methods were passed down, how modules added behavior, and how built-in functions were really methods from Kernel. We checked out how Enumerable and Comparable made it easy to go through and compare things. By defining a single method like each or <=>, we unlocked operations like mapping, filtering, sorting, and checking ranges of data. This clarity meant that everyday tasks involving arrays, sets, and custom objects took fewer lines of code. Lastly, we finally got a new appreciation for regular expressions as we handled text matching and manipulation. Basically, we discovered that even the most complex string checks could be reduced to concise patterns, letting us validate or transform data at scale. Overall, we gained a sense of how Ruby's built-in classes and modules combined power and elegance to make everyday development simpler.

CHAPTER 9: WORKING WITH PROCS, LAMBDAS, AND ENUMERATORS

Chapter Overview

In this chapter, you'll learn how Ruby treats code as data by diving into Procs, lambdas, and enumerators. A Proc or lambda lets you capture a block of code and store it in a variable. This lets you pass logic around like any other object. You'll learn ways to invoke these closures at your convenience. That makes certain methods reusable and adaptable. You'll see slight differences in return behavior and argument checking between Procs and lambdas, which will help you write more modular solutions.

After that, you'll take a closer look at enumerators, learning how they chain multiple operations like map, select, or each_with_index with minimal overhead. It'll show you a streamlined style that cuts down on temporary arrays or complicated loops, and you'll see how Ruby's syntax encourages readable transformations across collections. Finally, you'll learn how to incorporate Proc objects to gain flexibility, blending these ideas to create code that respects separation of concerns and remains open to change. This perspective cultivates a more fluid style of programming that matches well with Ruby's emphasis on clarity and expressiveness.

Creating Procs and Lambdas

Introduction to Lambdas

A lambda in Ruby is similar to a block but wrapped in an actual **`Proc`** object, enabling you to store it in variables, pass it to multiple methods, or return it from functions. Lambdas check the number of arguments strictly and handle **`return`** in a more conventional way (returning from the lambda itself, not the enclosing method). You might create one by using the **`->`** syntax or the **`lambda`** keyword:

```
greeter = ->(name) { "Hello, #{name}!" }
puts greeter.call("Alice")  # => "Hello, Alice!"
adder = lambda { |x, y| x + y }
puts adder.call(10, 5)      # => 15
```

Here, **`greeter`** and **`adder`** store code that can be invoked at any time. Lambdas enforce argument counts, so calling **`adder.call(10)`** would result in an ArgumentError. Also, if you place a **`return`** inside the body of a lambda, it only exits the lambda rather than returning from the method enclosing it. This behavior contrasts with blocks, which can break out of the surrounding method if a **`return`** is used.

Exploring Procs

A Proc in Ruby can be seen as a more general form of a lambda, though lambdas themselves are technically a specialized type of Proc. You create one using **Proc.new** or the **proc** method:

```
greeter_proc = Proc.new { |name| "Hello from proc, #{name}!" }

puts greeter_proc.call("Bob") # => "Hello from proc, Bob!"

multiplier = proc { |x, y| x * (y || 1) } # y defaults to 1 if
omitted

puts multiplier.call(8)        # => 8 (y was nil, so y || 1 is
1)

puts multiplier.call(8, 2)     # => 16
```

Unlike lambdas, Procs do not strictly enforce the number of arguments. If fewer arguments are passed, the missing ones become **nil** (or you can apply a fallback in your code). A **return** inside a Proc tries to exit not just the Proc itself but also the enclosing method, which often surprises newcomers. Another subtlety is that you cannot always rely on a Proc's parameters to behave just like lambdas, especially if argument checking or local returns matter in your design. Despite these differences, Procs remain powerful for capturing code blocks that you can reuse, store, and manipulate.

Blocks, lambdas, and Procs perform similar roles but differ in usage and flexibility:

- **Blocks**: Light and inline, associated with a single method invocation. They cannot be passed around as objects without first converting them to a Proc. A **return** inside a block exits the surrounding method, and argument checks are not strict.
- **Lambdas**: They strictly check the number of arguments. A **return** inside a lambda only exits that lambda. This approach aligns better with typical function semantics in other languages.
- **Procs**: They are more general than lambdas. They are those objects that can be saved in variables or passed around. They do not strictly enforce argument counts, and a **return** can bubble up to exit the entire method scope.

If you want to capture code that enforces argument checks and uses **return** in a local sense, lambdas are a better fit. If you prefer something more flexible about arguments and can handle the implications of **return**, a standard Proc might be adequate. Blocks are perfect if you just need an inline snippet to pass once, though you lose the reusability that comes from a first-class object.

Sample Program: Putting Blocks, Lambdas and Procs into Action

Let us look at the below sample code that will take into account all of these objects together in action:

```
def demonstrate_code_variants
  # 1) Using a block directly
  result_block = [1, 2, 3].map { |n| n * 2 }
  puts "Block result: #{result_block.inspect}"  # => [2, 4, 6]
  # 2) Using a lambda
  doubler_lambda = ->(x) { x * 2 }
  result_lambda = [4, 5, 6].map(&doubler_lambda)
  puts "Lambda result: #{result_lambda.inspect}" # => [8, 10,
12]
  # 3) Using a proc
  doubler_proc = Proc.new { |x| x * 2 }
  result_proc = [7, 8, 9].map(&doubler_proc)
  puts "Proc result: #{result_proc.inspect}"     # => [14, 16,
18]
  # Argument checking example
  puts "Lambda check:"
  triple_lambda = ->(x, y) { x * y }
  begin
    puts triple_lambda.call(3) # ArgumentError
  rescue => e
    puts "Error in lambda: #{e.message}"
  end
  puts "Proc check:"
  triple_proc = proc { |x, y| x * (y || 1) }
  puts triple_proc.call(3)      # => 3, no error
end
demonstrate_code_variants
```

In the above sample program, each approach returns a new array from **map**. We can notice how converting a block to an object requires the **&** operator, tying the block or lambda or proc to the method that processes it. Meanwhile, you see lambdas raise an **ArgumentError** for missing parameters, while the proc simply substitutes **nil** (or a default) without error. Such outcomes reflect the core differences among blocks, lambdas, and Procs, guiding your choice based on whether you need strictness or flexibility.

Chaining Operations with Enumerators

Ruby provides a strong set of iterator methods that enable you to transform, filter, or traverse collections without writing explicit loops. Sometimes, though, you need to apply multiple operations in sequence: for instance, you might want to select certain items, then map them to new values, and finally sort the results. Chaining these operations brings clarity by letting you combine them into one fluent series of calls, rather than forming numerous intermediate arrays. This approach saves memory, makes the logic more readable, and highlights Ruby's functional style of data transformation. While the typical enumerator methods like **map** or **select** produce arrays, Ruby also offers lazy enumeration, in which data is processed in a stream-like manner. That approach is invaluable for large datasets or infinite sequences. However, even with regular enumerators, chaining fosters an elegant workflow that helps isolate and verify each step.

Setting up Chained Calls

Following is a quick demonstration with arrays might look like this:

```
numbers = [1, 2, 3, 4, 5, 6]
result = numbers
  .select { |n| n.even? }         # Grab even numbers
  .map { |n| n * 2 }              # Double them
  .sort                           # Sort ascending
puts "Chained result: #{result.inspect}"  # => [4, 8, 12]
```

Here, the array flows through each method in turn. First, **select** filters out elements, returning only even ones. Next, **map** doubles each of those numbers. Finally, **sort** reorders the list. By chaining these, you avoid building multiple temporary variables like **evens = ...**, **doubled = ...**, and so on. Instead, you get a succinct expression that reads like a pipeline of transformations. If you wanted to only keep values above 6, you could tack on another call as below:

```
filtered = numbers
  .select { |n| n.even? }
  .map { |n| n * 2 }
```

```ruby
  .reject { |n| n <= 6 }
puts "Further filtered: #{filtered.inspect}"  # => [8, 12]
```

This style matches Ruby's approach of showing the transformations in a method chain, with each step producing an enumerator or a final array.

Sample Program: Applying Enumerators in Complex Case

Suppose we have a group of users that includes both **AdminUser** and **GuestUser**:

```ruby
all_users = [
  AdminUser.new("Alice", 35, :active, 2),
  GuestUser.new("Bob", 25, :inactive),
  AdminUser.new("Carol", 40, :active, 3),
  GuestUser.new("Dave", 20, :inactive)
]
# Suppose we want to find the names of all admin users over
30, sorted alphabetically
admin_names = all_users
  .select { |u| u.is_a?(AdminUser) }
  .select { |admin| admin.age > 30 }
  .map { |admin| admin.name }
  .sort
puts "Admin users over 30: #{admin_names.inspect}"
```

Here, by tacking on multiple **select** calls, you filter step by step: first ensuring the user is an **AdminUser**, then checking if **age > 30**. Finally, **map** extracts names, and **sort** orders them. As a result, you get a readable pipeline that's easy to modify or debug. If performance or clarity calls for a single **select** block, you could combine conditions, but in some scenarios, multiple steps highlight each filtering layer.

Lazy Enumeration

By default, methods like **map** and **select** return arrays, applying transformations right away. However, if your data is very large or even infinite, you could use lazy enumerators to avoid generating massive intermediate arrays. Lazy enumeration evaluates each step as items are accessed, not all at once. You trigger it by calling **lazy** on an enumerator before chaining:

```
numbers = (1..Float::INFINITY).lazy  # An infinite range
result = numbers
  .select { |n| n.even? }
  .map { |n| n * 2 }
  .take(5)     # Only take 5 elements from this infinite
pipeline
  .to_a
puts "Lazy chain result: #{result.inspect}"  # => [4, 8, 12,
16, 20]
```

While an infinite range is a bit contrived, it demonstrates how you can handle large inputs. Each item flows through the pipeline, and once enough items are produced (here, 5), iteration stops. That design prevents the program from attempting to process an unbounded quantity of data in one go. For typical day-to-day tasks, standard enumerators suffice. However, if you process large logs or streaming inputs, lazy enumerators let you chain transforms without loading everything into memory at once.

Sample Program: Extending Enumerators

Let's say you have an array of temperature readings and want to do a multi-step transformation:

```
temperatures = [36.5, 37.2, 38.9, 39.1, 36.8, 37.6]
processed = temperatures
  .select { |t| t <= 39.0 }                # Exclude readings above
39.0
  .map { |t| t.round(1) }                  # Round to one decimal
place
  .uniq                                    # Remove duplicates
  .sort
puts "Processed temperatures: #{processed.inspect}"
```

In one chain, you define the logic for filtering high readings, rounding them off, removing repeated values, and then sorting. Each step is separate but connected, forming a neat pipeline. If you had thousands of readings, you'd still get clarity in how you handle them, step by step, without manually writing loops or nested conditionals.

Debugging Chained Code

When enumerators are chained extensively, you might wonder how to debug or check intermediate steps. There is a way out and one of the approach is to break the chain with a local variable to see the result at each juncture:

```
temp_filtered = temperatures.select { |t| t <= 39.0 }
temp_rounded = temp_filtered.map { |t| t.round(1) }
unique_temps = temp_rounded.uniq
final_result = unique_temps.sort
puts "Final result: #{final_result.inspect}"
```

That style is less concise but sometimes more approachable during debugging. Another option is to insert a quick **tap** call that reveals intermediate states:

```
processed = temperatures
  .select { |t| t <= 39.0 }
  .tap { |arr| puts "After select: #{arr.inspect}" }
  .map { |t| t.round(1) }
  .tap { |arr| puts "After map: #{arr.inspect}" }
  .uniq
  .tap { |arr| puts "After uniq: #{arr.inspect}" }
  .sort
```

tap yields the object to your block, enabling you to log or inspect it without changing the chain.

Here, the result is not just shorter code but also a more meaningful, pipeline-like representation of data processing. When integrated into your existing program with its custom classes, enumerators ensure consistency and maintain the language's principle of clear, expressive solutions.

Leveraging Proc Objects for Flexibility

In the previous chapter, we learnt to define Proc once, then apply it in various contexts without rewriting the logic. This pattern aligns with a functional style, where methods can receive or return Procs that handle tasks such as data filtering, transformations, or conditional checks. Although similar to lambdas, Procs differ by not strictly enforcing argument counts and by how they handle

return statements. If you want more relaxed argument handling, Procs can suit that need perfectly.

Below is a quick example tying Procs into our earlier user-management context. Suppose you have multiple strategies for updating user data. Rather than creating separate methods for each approach, you can define them as Procs, then pass them to a method that processes users:

```
# procs_in_practice.rb
require_relative 'dynamic_demo'  # Contains User, AdminUser,
GuestUser, etc.
# A method that receives a proc for how to update a user
def process_user_with_strategy(user, update_proc)
  puts "Before update: Name=#{user.name},
Status=#{user.status}"
  update_proc.call(user)
  puts "After update: Name=#{user.name},
Status=#{user.status}"
  puts "-----"
end
# Define different strategies as Procs
promote_to_active = Proc.new do |u|
  if u.respond_to?(:update_status)
    u.update_status(:active)
  else
    puts "Cannot update status for this object."
  end
end
rename_to_upper = Proc.new do |u|
  if u.respond_to?(:name) && u.respond_to?(:age)
    new_name = "#{u.name.upcase}-#{u.age}"
    # For the sake of demonstration, assume we can set @name
    u.instance_variable_set("@name", new_name)
    puts "Renamed user to #{new_name}."
```

```
  else
    puts "Object cannot be renamed."
  end
end
begin
  admin_user = AdminUser.new("Alice", 35, :inactive, 2)
  guest_user = GuestUser.new("Bob", 25, :inactive)
  # Strategy 1: Promote user to active
  process_user_with_strategy(admin_user, promote_to_active)
  process_user_with_strategy(guest_user, promote_to_active)
  # Strategy 2: Rename user to uppercase plus age
  process_user_with_strategy(admin_user, rename_to_upper)
  process_user_with_strategy(guest_user, rename_to_upper)
rescue => e
  puts "An error occurred: #{e.message}"
end
```

Here in the above sample program, **promote_to_active** checks if the user supports the **update_status** method, then calls it with **:active**. You could extend it to log or perform validations. The **rename_to_upper** retrieves the user's name and age, then sets a new name by combining them.

You might notice that using a Proc can sometimes behave unexpectedly if the arguments differ or if you put a **return** statement within the block. Lambdas avoid that confusion by imposing stricter rules, aligning more closely with standard function calls. That said, Procs are often more forgiving in dynamic contexts, and some developers prefer the minimal fuss about argument counts. If your logic depends on consistent argument usage or a more typical **return**, lambdas might be safer. However, if you want to allow missing arguments or handle them gracefully, a Proc offers that flexibility out of the box.

Summary

We discovered that Ruby's block usage extended naturally into procs and lambdas, opening a realm of possibilities for dynamic code. Procs, as first-class objects, stored entire chunks of logic that could be passed around or reused, while lambdas enforced stricter argument checking and localized returns. Meanwhile, enumerators revealed a streamlined style of chaining operations like map, select, and reduce, culminating in succinct transformations across arrays and custom collections. This pipeline approach made things easier to read and cut down on extra code, encouraging a more functional style. The presence of enumerators also introduced lazy evaluation for large or infinite sequences, preserving memory and expanding beyond typical array usage.

We also saw how enumerators can be integrated with procs or lambdas, letting entire pipelines pass from one transformation to another without losing clarity. The result was a system of composable operations that took advantage of Ruby's emphasis on conciseness. By getting all these features under our belt, we can make dynamic code sections seem more natural and give more defined boundaries between data logic and iteration strategies.

Chapter 10: Up and Running with Gems

Chapter Overview

Welcome to the final chapter of your Ruby excursion. Here, we begin with exploring gems and libraries, starting with how to locate and install the packages, ensuring that your Ruby environment gains new capabilities with minimal fuss. You will see that gems are more than just standalone scripts: they often include documentation, executables, and well-tested functionalities ready to plug into your applications. By tapping into public repositories, you streamline your workflow, devoting energy to unique logic rather than re-creating libraries for tasks like data parsing or API requests. This perspective clarifies how gems align with Ruby's philosophy of collaboration and code sharing.

You will then understand and explore the RubyGems workflow, discovering how to manage versions and dependencies efficiently. A brief look at commands like **`gem install`**, **`gem list`**, or **`gem uninstall`** sheds light on routine operations that keep your environment tidy. Finally, you will get a hands-on overview of popular gems, illustrating why they remain common choices in everything from web frameworks to testing suites. With this, you will be prepared to harness the power of a vibrant open-source ecosystem without sacrificing stability or maintainability of your application.

Finding and Installing Gems

A gem is like a little package that adds extra stuff to your Ruby environment. They can be as small as a few utilities or as big as a full-featured framework. When you install a gem, you get more ways to use the language without having to make everything new yourself. Even though we've looked a lot at Ruby code in earlier chapters, we haven't really dealt with these community libraries or gems yet. Basically, gems cover everything from JSON and PDF parsing, to web frameworks like Rails. Each gem usually comes with code, documentation, and sometimes executables that integrate easily with the RubyGems system, so you can access all the community's work and keep things simple. This way of doing things captures Ruby's collaborative spirit, allowing you to stay focused on the unique aspects of your project.

How Gems fit the Ruby Ecosystem?

Ruby's packaging and distribution revolve around RubyGems. Each gem is uploaded to a central repository, often referred to as "rubygems.org," where others can retrieve it. This setup makes it easy to share and version your own libraries or rely on those published by others. By calling **`gem install gem_name`**, you fetch and install the code to your local environment. However, managing dozens of gems manually becomes cumbersome, so bundler steps in to automate version locking and dependency resolution. Bundler ensures that the same gem versions are used across machines and deployments, preventing conflicts or unexpected updates that might break your application.

Bundler for Dependency Management

Bundler is a widely used tool that reads a file named **Gemfile** to determine which gems you need, along with desired or compatible versions. By running **bundle install**, you let Bundler fetch these gems and store them in a local directory. This process removes guesswork, as each collaborator or environment uses the same gem set. The **Gemfile.lock** file (generated automatically) records exact versions, preventing surprise updates. This approach upholds consistency, so any stage from development to production sees matching behavior. For example, a partial Gemfile might look like:

```
# Gemfile
source "https://rubygems.org"
gem "sinatra"
gem "nokogiri"
gem "rspec"
```

When you run **bundle install**, Bundler downloads **sinatra**, **nokogiri**, **rspec**, and any transitive dependencies. Later, calling **bundle exec ruby my_script.rb** ensures your script uses the gems from that bundle rather than any conflicting global versions.

Installing Gems

Apart from bundler usage, RubyGems itself provides simple commands to find and install gems. For instance, running:

```
gem search nokogiri
```

searches RubyGems.org for "nokogiri," a popular gem for parsing HTML and XML. To install it:

```
gem install nokogiri
```

Once installed, **require "nokogiri"** in your Ruby code grants access to the gem's classes and methods. However, if you rely on many libraries, it's better to maintain a Gemfile and a consistent Bundler-driven workflow so that each project keeps a known set of dependencies.

Sample Program: Adding Gem to our Program

Suppose our sample program requires a gem for generating PDF reports based on user data. We could choose a gem like "prawn," a PDF generation library. Given below is a demonstration of how you might integrate it with bundler:

First, create or update the Gemfile in your project directory:

```
# Gemfile
source "https://rubygems.org"
gem "prawn", "~> 2.4"
```

Next, run the bundler to install dependencies:

```
bundle install
```

This downloads **prawn** and any required libraries, saving them locally. A new Gemfile.lock file is generated to lock the versions.

Now use the gem in your program script:

```
# pdf_demo.rb
require "bundler/setup"
Bundler.require(:default)
# The above lines ensure bundler loads gems in :default group
from Gemfile
require "prawn"
def generate_user_report(user)
  Prawn::Document.generate("#{user.name}_report.pdf") do |pdf|
    pdf.text "User Name: #{user.name}"
    pdf.text "Age: #{user.age}"
    pdf.text "Status: #{user.status}"
  end
  puts "PDF generated for #{user.name}"
end
# Sample usage with a user from our ongoing program
require_relative "dynamic_demo"  # hypothetical file with User
class
admin = AdminUser.new("Alice", 35, :active, 2)
generate_user_report(admin)
```

In the above, **prawn** is automatically available after Bundler sets the environment. The **require "prawn"** call loads the library, letting you generate PDFs. This snippet exemplifies how to incorporate a third-party gem into a real scenario. The result is a PDF file named **Alice_report.pdf** containing the user's details.

Now with the project growth, you might accumulate a dozen or more gems. Each gem might depend on others, forming a dependency graph. Bundler helps ensure that if gem A needs version 2.0 of gem B, you don't install version 3.0 that might introduce incompatible changes. The Gemfile can specify version constraints, such as **gem "rails", "~> 6.1"** or **gem "pg", ">= 1.1.4"**, instructing Bundler to pick the best matching versions. Whenever a new environment is set up (development or production), **bundle install** resolves everything exactly, letting you avoid "it works on my machine" confusion. If you choose to upgrade a gem, you can run **bundle update gem_name**, which re-resolves only that gem and its dependencies, adjusting the Gemfile.lock accordingly.

The other thing is that you may no longer need a gem or decide to switch libraries. If you installed gems globally with **gem install**, you can remove them with **gem uninstall gem_name**. For bundler-managed projects, simply remove the gem's line from the Gemfile and run **bundle install** again, which prunes the gem if it's not needed by other dependencies. This tidiness ensures that your code remains lean, depending only on libraries that remain relevant to your application.

In addition, if you want to upgrade all gems to the latest versions that still satisfy your constraints, a command like:

```
bundle update
```

fetches new releases. Alternatively, specifying a gem name, e.g., **bundle update nokogiri**, updates only that library. Reviewing release notes or running tests after each update is advisable, just in case an upgrade breaks existing behavior. This practice fosters a stable but not stagnant environment.

Hands-on with RubyGems Workflow

An introduction to gem creation starts with establishing a folder structure that neatly organizes your code and metadata. An individual might open a new directory with a name corresponding to the gem, then place a **lib** folder inside that holds the Ruby files. A typical gem includes a main file that mirrors the gem's name, so a gem called **my_sample_gem** would have **lib/my_sample_gem.rb** as a core file. A special file, often named **my_sample_gem/version.rb**, contains a **VERSION** constant. That constant helps the gem manager track incremental updates, letting everyone know whether they're working with **0.1.0**, **0.2.0**, or higher. A Gem specification, stored in a file called

my_sample_gem.gemspec, describes the gem, listing the name, version, authors, summary, and declared runtime or development dependencies. A typical specification references the **files** to be included, as well as any required Ruby version or gem prerequisites.

Following is a quick sample of a gem specification **my_sample_gem.gemspec**:

```
# my_sample_gem.gemspec
Gem::Specification.new do |spec|
  spec.name                  = "my_sample_gem"
  spec.version               = MySampleGem::VERSION
  spec.authors               = ["Your Name"]
  spec.email                 = ["your_email@example.com"]
  spec.summary               = "A short description of this gem."
  spec.description           = "A longer explanation of what this gem
does."
  spec.homepage              =
"https://github.com/your_username/my_sample_gem"
  spec.license               = "MIT"
  spec.files                 = Dir["lib/**/*.rb"]
  spec.required_ruby_version = ">= 2.7"
  spec.add_dependency "some_other_gem", "~> 1.0"
end
```

A user can define **MySampleGem::VERSION** in **lib/my_sample_gem/version.rb**:

```
# lib/my_sample_gem/version.rb
module MySampleGem
  VERSION = "0.1.0"
end
```

A reference to this version constant in the gemspec ensures that bumping the number in **version.rb** automatically updates the gem's specification. That approach keeps the version's definition in a single place, avoiding confusion. When everything is set, a developer can run **gem build my_sample_gem.gemspec**, which creates a **.gem** package. This artifact is the compressed library that can be installed locally or pushed to RubyGems.org. If one wants to test it locally, a quick **gem install ./my_sample_gem-0.1.0.gem** (adjusting the file name to match the built gem) places the library in the local environment. After installation, a simple **require "my_sample_gem"** from any Ruby script or IRB session should load the gem's functionalities. That test stage validates that the gem is structurally sound before sharing it more broadly.

A push to RubyGems.org typically begins by creating an account on that site, then generating an API key. A developer places that key in their environment or a credentials file so the gem command can authenticate. A single command, **gem push my_sample_gem-0.1.0.gem**, uploads the gem, making it available for others to install using standard RubyGems workflow. The server indexes the gem, associating it with your account. From that point forward, you can type **gem install my_sample_gem** to fetch and install the library on your systems. When you increment the version to **0.2.0** in your gem's version file and build a new **.gem**, another push replaces the older release with the new version, allowing existing projects to upgrade when they see fit. This versioning approach, backed by semantic versioning norms, helps maintain clarity about how updates might affect compatibility or introduce new features.

Working with Popular Gems

Setting up Nokogiri and Faker

A couple of widely used gems in the Ruby ecosystem are Nokogiri and Faker. We have already learned installing Nokogiri in the earlier topic but we will do it again for the sake of practising it. This Nokogiri specializes in parsing and manipulating HTML or XML, while Faker generates mock data for tasks like testing or populating fields with random details.

Now, to incorporate these gems into your project, you can add them to your **Gemfile**:

```
# Gemfile
source "https://rubygems.org"
gem "nokogiri"
gem "faker"
```

After saving this file, run:

```
bundle install
```

This fetches Nokogiri and Faker, along with any dependencies they require. When you want to leverage them in your code, a simple **require "nokogiri"** or **require "faker"** will expose their functionality. For convenience, if Bundler is managing your environment, you might add:

```
require "bundler/setup"
Bundler.require
```

in your main script so that the installed gems become immediately available. This approach eases usage in both local development and deployment settings.

Parsing HTML with Nokogiri

Nokogiri shines when you need to scrape or transform markup. Suppose you have an HTML snippet capturing user data. You can parse it to extract relevant fields or restructure it. We will now demonstrate a small script that loads an HTML fragment and prints out certain elements:

```
# parse_html_demo.rb
require "nokogiri"
html_content = <<-HTML
<!DOCTYPE html>
<html>
  <head><title>Sample Data</title></head>
  <body>
    <div class="user-profile">
      <h2 class="name">Alice</h2>
      <p class="age">35</p>
      <p class="status">active</p>
    </div>
    <div class="user-profile">
      <h2 class="name">Bob</h2>
      <p class="age">25</p>
      <p class="status">inactive</p>
    </div>
  </body>
</html>
HTML
```

```
doc = Nokogiri::HTML(html_content)
profiles = doc.css(".user-profile")
profiles.each do |profile|
  name = profile.at_css(".name").text
  age = profile.at_css(".age").text.to_i
  status = profile.at_css(".status").text
  puts "Found user: Name=#{name}, Age=#{age},
Status=#{status}"
end
```

In the above script,

- **`Nokogiri::HTML(html_content)`** parses the string and returns a **`Nokogiri::HTML::Document`** object.
- We use **`doc.css(".user-profile")`** to select all elements with class **`user-profile`**.
- Within each profile, **`profile.at_css(".name").text`** locates the user's name. A call to **`.text`** returns the textual content.
- Because **`.age`** might represent a numeric detail, you could convert it to an integer.

If you wanted to integrate the extracted data with the rest of your sample program, you might create new **`User`** or **`AdminUser`** instances. For example, if **`status`** is **`"active"`**, you might instantiate an **`AdminUser`**, else you'd choose a **`GuestUser`**. This snippet underscores how succinctly Nokogiri can handle HTML, freeing you from writing custom parsing loops or regex-based logic.

Generating Data with Faker

Faker provides a wide selection of methods to produce random but believable data: names, emails, phone numbers, addresses, etc. Such data can fill forms during testing, seed databases for development environments, or supply plausible user attributes without revealing real information.

Following is a quick example:

```
# faker_demo.rb
require "faker"
# Generate a random name and some other details
```

```
random_name = Faker::Name.name
random_email = Faker::Internet.email
random_address = Faker::Address.full_address
puts "Generated name: #{random_name}"
puts "Generated email: #{random_email}"
puts "Generated address: #{random_address}"
# Suppose you want to create dummy user objects for testing
dummy_users = 5.times.map do
  name = Faker::Name.name
  age  = rand(18..70)
  status = [:active, :inactive, :banned].sample
  { name: name, age: age, status: status }
end
puts "Dummy users:"
dummy_users.each { |du| puts du.inspect }
```

Here, **Faker::Name.name** returns a random full name. **Faker::Internet.email** conjures an email structure such as "john.doe@example.com". And the **Faker::Address.full_address** yields an address with street, city, and ZIP.

In a more integrated scenario, you might feed these details into your **User** or **AdminUser** classes, simulating a small population for demonstration or test runs.

Sample Program: Integrating Nokogiri and Faker

Let us consider a scenario wherein our application tracks users or processes reading logs, so here we might combine Nokogiri and Faker. For example, a developer might do something like this:

```
require "faker"
require "nokogiri"
dummy_users = 3.times.map do
  name   = Faker::Name.name
  age    = rand(20..60)
  status = [:active, :inactive].sample
```

```
  { name: name, age: age, status: status }
end
html_list = <<-HTML
<html>
<body>
#{dummy_users.map do |du|
  <<-CHUNK
  <div class="user-profile">
    <h2 class="name">#{du[:name]}</h2>
    <p class="age">#{du[:age]}</p>
    <p class="status">#{du[:status]}</p>
  </div>
  CHUNK
end.join}
</body>
</html>
HTML
doc = Nokogiri::HTML(html_list)
profiles = doc.css(".user-profile")
profiles.each do |profile|
  extracted_name   = profile.at_css(".name").text
  extracted_age    = profile.at_css(".age").text.to_i
  extracted_status = profile.at_css(".status").text
  puts "Parsed: Name=#{extracted_name}, Age=#{extracted_age},
Status=#{extracted_status}"
end
```

Here in the above code, the **Faker** generates a small list of random user attributes. The code dynamically inserts them into an HTML template. And the **Nokogiri** parses that generated HTML, confirming the script can extract the same details.

This above example demonstrates how both gems can collaborate, replicating a micro workflow where data is produced, embedded in markup, and extracted again.

Summary

So, to sum it up, we learned that using RubyGems lets our programs use existing libraries without a lot of complexity. By declaring dependencies in a Gemfile and running Bundler, we could get the packages we needed while making sure the versions were consistent across different environments. We also learned how to create a gem and organize the files in a way that's easy to predict, set a version constant, and list the gem dependencies in the gemspec.

Then, we looked at some popular gems like Nokogiri and Faker, and you got to do hands-on stuff like parsing HTML or generating random data, which saved you time when getting ready for tests or dealing with user input. The tight integration with Bundler and RubyGems gave you a universal workflow for installation, updates, and removal. You can handle multiple gems, manage locked versions, and publish your own packages. This makes your code more portable, reusable, and stable. All of these features work together to give you a more versatile environment where you can quickly adopt proven libraries to support your evolving requirements.

Index

Epilogue

Now that we're wrapping up this book, I hope you feel like you've really accomplished something and are all set to dive into your own Ruby projects with confidence. In this book, we've gone through all the ins and outs of Ruby, turning theoretical ideas into real-world skills that let you build solid and fast applications. You've got the hang of writing clean, reusable code using blocks, procs, and lambdas, which really shows off Ruby's expressive syntax. You've also learned to handle complex data transformations effortlessly by diving into enumerators, making your programs powerful and elegant. You've also learned to use RubyGems to add community libraries like Nokogiri and Faker to your projects. This lets you focus on what really matters—solving unique problems and delivering value through your apps.

And you can optimize performance like a pro. With the benchmarking techniques you've picked up, you can spot and get rid of bottlenecks, making sure your Ruby apps run smoothly and efficiently even under tough conditions. And with the know-how you've gained, you can now package your apps into executables and gems, making it a breeze to distribute your work. You can reach users and customers without any of the usual hassle of complicated installations or dependency issues. You've got the skills to use version control, specifically Git, in your workflow. You know how to track changes, work with others, and keep your project history neat and tidy. This base is key to getting more done, but also makes sure your projects stay manageable and easy to grow.

You'll be able to take on all kinds of projects, from simple scripts to complex web applications, thanks to the knowledge you'll gain from this book. You're now ready to tackle challenges with a strategic mindset, using best practices in debugging, performance optimization, and dependency management to build applications that will last. But this is just the start. The Ruby ecosystem is always changing, with new gems, tools, and methodologies popping up all the time. Your journey doesn't end here; it continues as you apply what you've learned, experiment with new ideas, and contribute to the vibrant Ruby community. You could develop innovative web applications, automate tasks, or create libraries that others will find invaluable. No matter what you choose to do, the foundation you built with "Practical Ruby 3 Programming" will support you every step of the way.

Thanks so much for having me along for the ride. I'm pumped to see the awesome Ruby apps you'll build and the positive impact they'll have. So, go ahead, embrace the power of Ruby, keep learning, and let your creativity shine through every line of code you write.

Cheers to your ongoing success in the Ruby programming world!

— Zorin Fylix

Thank You

Thank You

www.ingramcontent.com/pod-product-compliance
Lightning Source LLC
Chambersburg PA
CBHW080216170726
48282CB00030B/1136